Reader's Digest

Vegetarian
COOKBOOK

Reader's Digest

Vegetarian

COOKBOOK

Published by the Reader's Digest Association Ltd
London • New York • Sydney • Montreal

Why eat vegetarian?

In the UK today, around five per cent of the population consider themselves to be vegetarians, following a diet that excludes fish, meat and any animal by-products. A smaller proportion follow the far stricter vegan diet which excludes eggs and dairy produce too.

Some people choose vegetarianism because they are concerned about the welfare of animals raised for meat and the environmental consequences of meat production. Some want more complete information about the origin of their food. Others simply feel better eating an exclusively vegetarian diet.

Over the past 40 years the growing popularity of vegetarian cooking has been reflected in an ever more exiting range of recipes and produce. Here you will find more than 150 recipes, from light brunches to filling main courses and delectable desserts to inspire you to experiment with your vegetarian cooking.

BREAKFAST AND BRUNCH

STARTERS AND SNACKS

SOUPS

SALADS

ON THE SIDE

Protein

Fats

Minerals

a balanced

As long as you eat a good variety of foods in the correct proportions you should be able to achieve a healthy, balanced vegetarian diet. The basic rules are very simple – and apply whether or not you are following a vegetarian lifestyle. For general good health eat plenty of complex carbohydrates, a wide variety of fruit and vegetables and a small amount of protein. Add milk and dairy products for calcium (or their soya equivalents if you are vegan) but restrict saturated fat, salt and sugar.

CARBOHYDRATES

Around half of your daily energy, or calories, should come from carbohydrates – but they should be the complex kind; starchy foods such as brown rice, potatoes, and wholemeal bread or pasta. These kinds of foods will make you feel full, keep you satisfied for longer and provide you with a sustained source of energy. This last is particularly useful when doing sport or other energetic physical activity. Though sugary foods are also a source of carbohydrate, they tend to be calorie-rich with little other nutritional benefit. Restrict cakes, biscuits and other 'empty calorie' carbohydrates to special treats.

FIBRE

Fibre stimulates the digestive system and helps to prevent constipation, bowel disease, heart disease and many other health problems. Add fibre with a variety of wholegrains including oats as well as plenty of fruit and vegetables.

Vitamins

Carbohydrates

diet

THE GLYCAEMIC INDEX
The lower the GI (glycaemic index) of a food, the more slowly it is digested and glucose released into the bloodstream. Low or medium GI foods will keep you fuller for longer and avoid the urge to snack.

PROTEIN
Dairy products, eggs, tofu, pulses and nuts are good sources of protein which is needed for growth and repairing cells. The body does not need a lot of protein; around 45g a day is sufficient for most women with 55g as a good average for men. Protein foods also contain valuable minerals such as iron, zinc and magnesium.

FATS
A small amount of fat makes food taste better and provides essential fatty acids and fat-soluble vitamins. Fat should form around a third of a daily healthy diet. Current guidelines recommend cutting down on saturated fats as much as possible – not difficult with a vegetarian diet as most are found in meat and dairy foods. Mono-unsaturated fat, found in nuts, olive oil, groundnut oil and avocados is a healthier source.

VITAMINS
Essential chemicals, vitamins are required by the body in small quantities to help repair and development and synthesise other nutrients. Raw fruit and vegetables tend to retain vitamins better as cooking can break down certain kinds of vitamins – particularly those from the B and C groups.

MINERALS
The body contains a number of minerals, around 20 of which are thought to be essential. Some, such as calcium are needed in quite large quantities – over 100mg a day. Others are known as trace minerals but are still important, although only required in small amounts.

◄ 1 medium apple

3 whole dried apricots ►

▼ 1 medium banana

▲ 3 heaped tablespoons of carrots

◄ 2 broccoli florets

▼ 1 handful of grapes

▲ 3 heaped tablespoons of sweetcorn

half a large ► courgette

7 cherry ▼ tomatoes

▲ 7 strawberries

five a day

Current government advice is that everyone should eat at least five portions (400g) of fruit and vegetables a day. Each of the pictures shown above represents one of the five servings. But there is no harm in eating more than this and it is positively beneficial to eat as varied a range as possible. It has been estimated that if everyone tried to eat their 'five a day' the risk of deaths from chronic diseases such as heart disease, stroke, and cancer could be cut by as much as 20 per cent. A recent study found that each portion of fruit and vegetables reduced the risk of heart disease by four per cent and stroke by six per cent. Other benefits may include delaying the onset of cataracts, reducing the symptoms of asthma and improving the management of diabetes.

◀ 2 halves of canned peaches

2 satsumas ▶

▲ 3 heaped tablespoons of cooked kidney beans

1 tablespoon of raisins ▶

3 heaped ▶ tablespoons of peas

◀ 12 chunks of canned pineapple

1 medium glass of ▶ orange juice

▲ 1 handful of vegetable sticks

◀ 16 okra

1 medium pear ▶

The government, along with the World Health Organization, recommends **that everyone eats** at least **five** portions of fresh vegetables and fruit every day.

vegetables...

Vegetables are packed with vitamins and minerals. They also contain complex compounds known as phytochemicals. Some of these are antioxidants which can destroy free radicals and so have a protective role against cancer – as well as other harmful effects. They are also one of the best sources of minerals including iron, calcium, potassium, magnesium and folate and the vitamins A, B, C and E. You will get far more nutritional benefit from eating vegetables for vitamins and minerals than you will from taking them as a supplement. Low in fat, calories and cholesterol, vegetables are also an excellent source of dietary fibre – they will fill you up and keep your digestive system working smoothly.

BRASSICAS
Packed with minerals and vitamin C, brassicas include cabbage, kale, cauliflower and the super food broccoli.

BROCCOLI
Good in stir-fries, with pasta, in soufflés or quiches. Remove coarse leaves before cooking and peel back woody stems. Raw or steamed broccoli will retain most nutrients.

CABBAGE
Green cabbage is related to kale and has loose outer leaves. White and red cabbage are more tightly packed. White and red cabbage work well as salads, while kale and green cabbage can be lightly steamed and served with butter as a side dish.

BRUSSEL SPROUTS
More strongly flavoured than cabbage, they are generally eaten lightly cooked, although they can be used for salad. Remove outer leaves and cut a cross in the steam to help sprouts cook more quickly.

FENNEL SEEDS

Aromatic fennel seeds are one of the world's oldest spices. Traditional medicines have used a fennel-based tea to help a range of digestive problems from hiccups to colic. Fennel tea can also help to ease flatulence and bloating. In India, toasted fennel seeds are chewed after a meal to prevent bad breath and aid digestion. In ancient Greece and Rome, the seeds were eaten to prevent obesity. A teaspoon of cooled, weak fennel tea can be used as gripe-water for infants.

For too long relegated to a side dish, vegetables are finally being appreciated for their own flavour and texture, and most importantly, for their terrific health benefits.

CAULIFLOWER
Works well in curries and with cheese and cream sauces. Remove outer leaves and cut into florets before cooking. Slice stems thinly so they will cook more quickly.

LEAFY GREENS
Not always green, hues range from red or purple to dark bottle green.

SPINACH AND CHARD
Both work well in salads and soups. If using as an accompaniment, steam lightly in minimal water. Because they release so much water, you can expect the quantity to reduce by about half.

ORIENTAL GREENS
Loose leaved, they can be used in stir-fries and the young leaves in oriental salads. When preparing, chop the central rib and leaf separately.

STALKS AND BUDS
From artichokes to chicory, by way of asparagus, flavours range from delicate to more nutty or bitter.

GLOBE ARTICHOKE
A good source of folate and potassium, serve hot or cold, with its leaves stripped down to the heart. To eat whole, cut off the top and boil in salted water for 30-40 minutes. The leaves should come away when pulled gently. Serve with vinaigrette or melted butter.

ASPARAGUS
Delicately flavoured and tender at its best, asparagus was traditionally boiled upright in a tall saucepan. It is also wonderful grilled, roasted or stir-fried.

CELERY
Great as a flavouring for soups and casseroles, celery also adds a crunchy 'bite' to salads and stir fries.

FENNEL
Use the aniseed flavour of fennel to accompany Italian ingredients such as tomatoes and basil or citrus fruits, apples and pears. Slice thinly for salads or grill, roast or steam.

Most vegetables can be eaten raw - if you prefer them cooked, microwave or steam to keep the nutrients.

...vegetables

SALAD VEGETABLES
The ultimate raw food, salad vegetables don't need cooking to be at their best.

LETTUCE
Ring the changes with mild butterhead lettuce or lollo rosso or the crisper cos. Lamb's lettuce is more succulent, while feuille de chêne adds a touch of attractive colour.

CUCUMBER
Mainly water, cucumber is a refreshing ingredient. It works well chopped in a yoghurt dip or sliced into sticks for dipping.

AVOCADO
Actually a fruit, but with a delicate nutty flavour, avocadoes have a high fat content. It is healthy monunsaturated fat though. Eat with a vinaigrette dressing or chop and add to salads. Ripe avocadoes will yield slightly when pressed and should peel with ease. Sprinkle with lemon juice when cut to stop them from going black.

RADISH
Little bulbs with crimson or white roots, radishes add a peppery flavour to salads.

MUSHROOMS
Eaten in quantity, mushrooms can be a good source of potassium and trace elements. But they tend to be used for taste and texture rather than nutrition.

FRESH OR DRY
Dried fungi have a more intense flavour than their fresh counterparts.

They need to be soaked before use: rinse, cover with boiling water and stand for half an hour. Fresh mushrooms should be wiped.

BUTTON
These young mushrooms are ideal for salads, marinades and stir-fries.

CHESTNUT
With a dense texture and stronger flavour, chestnut mushrooms are a good addition to stews, stronger-flavoured sauces, nut roasts and pie fillings.

continued

CEP AND PORCINI
The French cep and Italian porcini are closely related. Available fresh or dried they have a woody flavour.

SHIITAKE
Originally a wild native of Japan, it has a chewy texture and a strong flavour. Slice thinly for sauces and stir-fries and use in chunky pieces in casseroles.

PORTOBELLO
Substantial flat mushrooms that can be used as a base for a range of toppings. Grill, roast, stuff or bake – or wrap in foil for the barbecue.

BEANS, PEAS AND SWEETCORN
Colourful and crunchy, all are best at their freshest – although frozen versions are just as nutritious.

PEAS
Make the most of the short summer season for fresh peas. Choose smooth, unblemished pods, then pop the peas and lightly boil, steam or microwave. Tiny fresh peas can be eaten raw.

MANGETOUT
Edible pods containing immature peas, they add colour and crunch to salads and stir fries. Sugar snaps are the plumper versions.

BEANS
Green beans add colour to stews and casseroles and go well with Mediterranean vegetables such as tomatoes, olives and peppers. When served alone they should be crisp and tender.

BROAD BEANS
Serve these substantial and nutritious beans with grain dishes such as paella and in garlicky salads.

SWEETCORN
Naturally sweet and delicious in all its forms. Use as tiny cobs in stir fries, cooked as corn on the cob or as kernels added to stews, grain dishes or salads. Sharp flavours such as lime or chilli add a bit of bite.

Try to vary the vegetables you **include in your 'five a day'** to get the maximum range of nutrients.

...vegetables

ROOT VEGETABLES
Hearty and filling in soups and stews, root vegetables can be used in a huge variety of other ways.

CARROTS
Crunchy and sweet raw, carrots are a good source of beta carotene and dietary fibre. They are also excellent cooked in soups or as chunky pieces in casseroles too.

POTATOES
Use waxy potatoes for salads and floury potatoes for baking and mashing. They are a good source of starchy energy.

SWEET POTATOES AND YAMS
Their orange or white sweet-flavoured flesh, adds interest to casseroles and roast well. Yams are more starchy than sweet potatoes and are good in mashes.

PARSNIP
With a sweet, strong flavour, parsnips are excellent roasted and make fantastic soup. They can be woody when older and should not be eaten raw.

TURNIP
The best turnips are small and white with a greenish or purple tinge. They have a delicate peppery flavour. Young turnips don't need to be peeled. They can be used in casseroles, in mashes, steamed, sautéed or stir-fried.

BEETROOT
Sweet and earthy, beets come in golden as well as red varieties. Scrub well, boil for 35 to 40 minutes and then peel. Or roast or bake. They taste good cold in salads and are ideal for pickling.

JERUSALEM ARTICHOKE
Tasting a bit like water chestnuts, they are good in stews and soups and with cream or spices. Scrub and peel if necessary before cooking.

CELERIAC
A knobbly, warty plant, with a delicate celery flavour. Good raw in salads, cooked in wine or puréed with soft cheese.

SWEDE
Peel to expose the yellow flesh and roast, steam or microwave for maximum flavour.

CHILLIES

From mild to searingly hot, chillies add piquancy to a wide range of dishes. Mild sweet chillies make a delightful salad dish when roasted and skinned. Place in the oven or under a grill and cook until the skin chars. The skin should come away easily; if not, place it in a plastic bag for ten minutes. When preparing chillies never touch your eyes or mouth.

continued

FRUIT VEGETABLES

The colourful savoury 'fruits' of a variety of plants, this diverse group lends itself to a variety of cooking methods.

SWEET PEPPERS

Mild relations of the spicy chilli with a mild, sweet flavour. Excellent raw in salads, they can be stuffed, baked and roasted. Like all bright red or orange vegetables they are good sources of antioxidants.

AUBERGINE

A staple of Mediterranean, especially Greek and Turkish cooking, they should feel glossy and heavy. Roast and purée or bake to prepare for inclusion in a moussaka.

COURGETTES

Do not skin. Wipe or rinse and chop large specimens. They can be stuffed, grilled, stir-fried, steamed lightly or marinaded for salads.

BUTTERNUT SQUASH

Use to add substance to casseroles or for colourful soups, or bake whole. They are good with cheese and strong spices or herbs to add flavour.

TOMATOES

Cherry or beefsteak work well raw in salads. while plum tomatoes are better for pulping to use in sauces and soups. Canned or sun-dried tomatoes are excellent for most cooking.

ONIONS

A key base flavouring for many dishes, onions may help to lower cholesterol levels and reduce the effect of fatty foods on the blood.

ONIONS AND SHALLOTS

Use sweet or red onions in salads. 'Sweating' onions gives the flavour base for many soups and casseroles.

GARLIC

Adds a pungent flavour to a diverse range of cuisines. Chop or crush and be careful not to burn when cooking or it will become bitter.

LEEKS

When cooked slowly leeks develop a delicate buttery texture. They are delicious with cheese and potatoes, in pies bakes and soups.

Keep a bowl of **apples, pears or peaches** close to hand as a **healthy snack.** And buy berries in season when they are best value and full of flavour.

fruit...

Gorgeously colourful, sweetly juicy and deliciously perfumed, there's a fruit for every taste. Make the most of local fruits in season as well as the exotic varieties now widely available. Most fruits are an important source of Vitamin C, which cannot be stored in the body and needs a daily top-up. Orange-fleshed fruits including apricots, peaches and mangoes also contain antioxident carotenes. You'll get the maximum nutritional benefit from the freshest fruit eaten raw. But as well as desserts and snacks, it's worth incorporating fruit into savoury dishes as well – apricots and dates will impart a middle eastern flavour to grain and rice-based recipes.

ORCHARD FRUIT
Delicious raw, apples and pears can also be cooked in a variety of ways for simple desserts.

APPLES
Apples are a good source of vitamin C, fibre and bioflavonoids. Use cooking apples such as Bramleys for pies and sauces. Tart, crisp apples generally work best for cooking.

PEARS
With plenty of natural sugars, pears are a good energy-boosting food.

They are also great stewed, grilled or poached.

STONE FRUIT
Soft-fleshed with a large central stone, most are are a good source of vitamin C and fibre so may aid digestion.

APRICOTS
Delicious dried, but also raw when completely ripe and poached for pies and crumbles.

PEACHES
Buy firm, but not rock hard and ripen in a

star performer...

BLUEBERRIES: A SUPER FRUIT

Naturally sweet, blueberries don't need cooking or sugar to make them palatable. Traditionally used to cure diarrhoea and food poisoning, blueberries contain anthocyansides which have antibacterial properties. They are a valuable aid against urinary tract infections such as cystitis and may also help to arrest deteriorating eyesight.

warm place. Poach, barbecue, grill or stew and purée.

PLUMS
Black, red, purple and yellow, some are grown specially for eating fresh while others are best cooked. Brilliant in crumbles and pies and dried as prunes

CHERRIES
Naturally sweet, they are wonderful raw when in season. Also good in cakes or muffins or as purées and sauces.

GRAPES
Actually a vine fruit, grapes are at their best eaten raw and perfectly fresh. Darker varieties have a natural bloom.

BERRIES
Pick your own from the garden or a farm for the freshest seasonal berries. Strawberries and raspberries can be puréed without cooking.

STRAWBERRIES
Rich in antioxidants they accompany most other fruits well. Fresh

fools, yoghurts and home-made icecream are a refreshing summer treat.

RASPBERRIES
Always eat as soon as possible as raspberries are delicate and perishable. Buy frozen for purées.

BLACK AND REDCURRANTS
Tartly flavoured, these tiny berries are an excellent topping for sweet, creamy desserts such as cheesecake. They are also packed with vitamin C.

CRANBERRIES
One of the superfruits, cranberries make a refreshing juice and excellent sauce for savouries. They may help to prevent urinary tract infections.

GOOSEBERRIES
Pale green or deep red, gooseberries need to be cooked and sweetened. They make good sauces and creamy fools.

All fruit is good for us, be it fresh, frozen, dried or canned.

HEALTHY DESSERTS

Fruit is most beneficial when eaten raw. Combining a number of fruits in a fresh fruit salad is a simple way to achieve several portions of your 'five a day' at one go. Prepare fruit salads at the last minute to keep them looking their best and retain maximum nutrients.

...fruit

CITRUS FRUITS

With thick, fragrant skin and juice-packed flesh, citrus fruits are more durable than most and are a superb source of vitamin C. Many are used for their juice. Citrus juice also stops many other fruit and vegetables from going brown when cut.

LEMON

Sharply flavoured, lemons make wonderful desserts when slightly sweetened and are also terrific used in savoury dishes for added zest.

ORANGE

Use bitter oranges such as the Seville for marmalade and cooking; sweet Valencia, naval and blood oranges for eating alone. Blood oranges are particularly good in fruit salads.

THE ORANGE FAMILY

Mandarins, tangerines, satsumas and clementines are related to oranges. Thinner-skinned and easier to peel, they are not generally used for cooking save as toppings or in fruit salad.

GRAPEFRUIT

Slightly sour, grapefruits make a refreshing juice. They can be segmented for use in fruit salads or lightly grilled for a starter or breakfast dish – sprinkle a cut half with sugar and place under a preheated grill for a few minutes.

KUMQUAT

Small oval fruits with an edible skin, they can be used as a garnish, with rice or couscous and in savoury salads.

TROPICAL FRUITS

A huge range of more exotic fruits is widely available. Use the best examples as available.

BANANA

A superb energy blast food, bananas make a quick snack and are a rich source of potassium. They are delicious baked or grilled and used chopped in cakes.

DATE

Eat alone or stuffed with a sweet or savoury filling. Use dried in

GETTING YOUR VITAMIN C

Many fruits are rich in vitamin C, vital for the production of collagen, an essential component of healthy skin, bones, cartilage, teeth and skin. It helps in healing wounds and burns and produces seratonin which regulates sleep. Vitamin C improves the iron uptake of vegetarians as the iron in plant foods is absorbed more efficiently when eaten with foods or fruit juices containing vitamin C.

continued

salads or Middle Eastern grain-based dishes.

FIG
The whole fruit is edible including the skin and seeds. The sweet, delicate flavour of fresh figs is great with cheese or dried. Dried figs are particularly high in fibre.

GUAVA
Mix the pulpy pink flesh with soft cheese as a dip or combine with apples or pears in a pie or crumble.

KIWI FRUIT
The furry exterior belies the tempting brilliant green interior. Kiwis have a vitamin C content higher than oranges and are good on their own, as elegant toppings or mixed with other fruits.

MANGO
The rich creamy flesh is great on its own or eaten with other fruits or in savoury salads. Mango is also renowned for its beneficial effects on the skin and kidneys.

MELON
Check a melon's ripeness by the sweetness of the smell. Combine with savouries or eat alone or in a fruit salad.

PAPAYA
With a yellow-green skin and pinky-orange flesh, papaya goes well with savouries such as chilli, coriander and avocado but is good on its own with a little lime juice.

PASSION FRUIT
Inside its tough wrinkled exterior are a golden pulp and hundreds of

edible seeds. Scoop out the seeds with a teaspoon or use the juice to flavour a fruit salad or fruit drink.

PINEAPPLE
Good in fruit salads and with savoury ingredients, pineapple can be grilled and barbecued and makes a lovely cake topping.

POMEGRANATE
Tightly-packed seeds are surrounded by red flesh. Divide into four, peel back the skin in sections to pull out the interior.

Supplying protein and many vitamins and minerals, in particular calcium, milk and other dairy products can play a vital role in maintaining good health.

dairy

Dairy products including milk, cheese and yoghurt are a familiar starting point for those new to a vegetarian diet. A good source of protein and calcium, cow's milk contains vitamins including A, B12 and D. Cheese in particular is high in saturated fat so should be eaten in moderation. Sheep and goats' milk products are also available and are an alternative for those who are sensitive to cow's milk. Eggs are also a great source of protein and are low in saturated fat. Choose free-range to ensure that they have been produced humanely. If you are looking for non-dairy alternatives, soya can be processed into milk, cheese and yoghurt, while tahini and tofu can be used instead of eggs.

MILK
Whole and semi-skimmed milk have a higher vitamin and mineral content than skimmed. Those who cannot tolerate cow's milk can try goat's milk instead.

CRÈME FRÂICHE
Rich, with a delicate tang it is good as a dressing and works well in soups and sauces.

YOGHURT
Made from cow's, ewe's and goat's milk and soya protein, yoghurt is available set and in a more runny version.

Delicious in savoury salad dressings and with fruit for desserts.

CHEESE
Unless you intend to be strictly vegan, it's hard to resist cheese. Choose varieties that are labelled as being suitable for vegetarians; this will ensure that they contain no rennet – an ingredient taken from a calf's stomach that is used to curdle and separate milk into curds and whey.

CHEDDAR
A firm-textured hard cheese; the mature

ALTERNATIVES TO DAIRY

Soya milk does not taste like cow's milk but is fine as a drink or on cereals. It is not ideal for sauces as it does tend to curdle. Soya cheese has the texture of processed cheese and can seem rather fatty. Tahini is a good binding agent instead of eggs for burgers and bakes but does curdle if you are not careful. Tofu can be used as an alternative to eggs in mayonnaise while silken tofu can be scrambled.

varieties will add lots of flavour to any sauce, though milder ones are fine for toppings.

PARMESAN
There is no vegetarian version of traditional Parmesan. But a variety of Parmesan-style hard cheeses which don't contain rennet are available.

GRUYÉRE
A Swiss cheese with small holes, it is good for grilling and melts well.

FETA
A sharp-flavoured ewe's milk cheese. Great in Mediterranean-style dishes and salads.

ROQUEFORT
A crumbly blue cheese made from ewe's milk.

STILTON
A classic English blue cheese, it should have a smooth, creamy texture. It is fantastic partnered with fresh figs.

BRIE
Look for a pale yellow centre which is soft but not runny. Good with fruit and in salads, but also delicious hot.

CHÈVRE
Goat's cheeses are strongly flavoured and make lovely starters grilled and served with vegetables or salad.

RICOTTA
A whey-based Italian soft cheese with a light texture, it is often used as a filling for ravioli.

FROMAGE FRAIS
A soft unripened cheese, its slightly sharp taste is often partnered with fruit in desserts.

MOZZARELLA
Firm-textured, it melts beautifully and is good with grilled vegetables and as a pizza topping.

EGGS
Store pointed end downwards to keep the yolk centred. Test for freshness by using the 'float' test; a fresh egg will sink. If using separated eggs, use yolks within a couple of days and whites within a week.

COOKING RICE AND WHOLEGRAINS

Bring a large saucepan of water to the boil. Add the grain and bring back to the boil then simmer gently until the grain is tender. Drain well. For risotto rice, millet and short-grain rice, use 1 litre stock for 250g grain. Add a third of the stock and bring to the boil, stirring constantly. When all the stock has been absorbed, repeat the process with the next third and finaly the last thrid of the stock. The whole process should take 20-30 minutes.

grains and

Cereals and grains are staples of many diets, from wheat, rye and barley in temperate zones to rice, maize and millet in more tropical climes. Wholegrains are seeds and contain a variety of valuable nutrients including carbohydrate, fibre, starch and essential amino acids. Once the grain is processed and the outer layer is cracked or removed, it begins to lose its nutritional value. Lesser known grains such as quinoa, buckwheat and wild rice offer exiting alternatives.

Pasta can made from any kind of flour and processed into a huge variety of shapes and sizes. Choose wholewheat pasta for slow-release energy and cook lightly to keep an authentic al dente texture.

WHOLEGRAINS

Grains are a rich source of essential amino acids, and eaten in conjunction with pulses or nuts will provide a complete vegetarian protein. They also contain valuable minerals.

BARLEY

One of the most ancient grains, barley today tends to be added to soups and casseroles.

MILLET

With a milder flavour than rice, the round grains of millet can be used for both sweet and savoury dishes.

QUINOA

Round grains with a delicate grassy flavour, make a good accompaniment for spicy vegetable dishes. Be careful not to overcook.

BUCKWHEAT

A flavoursome grain, it is sometimes known as kasha when toasted. Buckwheat goes well with root vegetables, mushrooms and dark green vegetables.

OATS

Used mainly in the form of meal or flakes, oats are the basis of muesli

THE GI FACTOR

Pasta is one of the best sources of slow-release carbohydrates – it's still recommended as being one of the best foods to eat the night before running a marathon. It is also low in fat and a useful source of protein. To get the maximum slow release energy from your pasta, it should be cooked until it is just beginning to soften, not until soft or soggy.

Grains, pasta and rice are some of the most versatile ingredients in a vegetarian diet. Always keep a selection in the storecupboard as an essential standby.

pasta

and porridge. The soluble dietary fibre they contain is thought to lower blood cholesterol.

RICE

Many different varieties arc now available. Keep a selection and choose the kind that best suits your recipe.

SHORT-GRAIN

The round sticky grains are suitable for savoury stuffings, puddings and risotto-style dishes.

LONG-GRAIN

Long-grain brown rice is nutty and good with chillies, stir-fries and curries.

BASMATI

Fragrant, with long, slender grains, it is a natural partner for curries and a range of other dishes.

RISOTTO

As the starch breaks down, the rice attains its creamy quality; varieties include Arborio and Carnaroli.

RED RICE

A Mediterranean rice with russet coloured grains that are nutty and chewy, it is good with other kinds of rice and with vegetables.

WILD RICE

The long slender grains are a dark brown and it has a nutty flavour which goes well with nuts and vegetables such as peppers and tomatoes.

WHEAT

BULGHUR

Made from cooked, dried and cracked whole wheat it just needs to be soaked in boiling water before using.

COUSCOUS

Made from the inner layers of the wheat, it can be lightly steamed or soaked in boiling water for 5 minutes.

PASTA

Keep pasta in a wide range of sizes, shapes and thicknesses. Added flavours such as tomato, spinach, basil, chilli and egg also add variety. Fine pastas are best with light, smooth sauces while shells, curls and broad noodles are usually better with more chunky sauces.

Almost all of the pulses contain **a near-perfect balance** of starchy carbohydrate and protein.

pulses and

Dried peas, beans and lentils are a cheap and nutritious alternative to meat. They contain protein, but not the amino acids essential for growth and the maintenance of healthy tissues. To get a good balance, serve with vegetables and whole grains such as rice or bread. Soya beans are the exception and are classed as a high-quality protein because they do contain amino acids. Pulses are also an excellent source of dietary fibre and generally have a low GI so will keep you full for longer. Nuts are a great source of energy. Though they are high in fat and calories, they contain essential fatty acids and are a good source of B vitamins which vegetarians may have difficulty in obtaining.

PULSES
Beans and lentils can be the basis for soups, stews and casseroles as well as burgers and savoury bakes. They will make a salad or a pasta sauce more substantial. And they are one of the cheapest forms of protein available.

BEANS
Dried beans have a long shelf life but should look plump and glossy, not wrinkled or cracked. Use black or kidney beans with chillies, mung beans with Indian spices,

cannellini beans with Mediterranean flavour and chickpeas for a Middle Eastern taste. To make beans more digestible, change the water during soaking, cook with spices such as cumin or caraway and try sprouting for a day or so before cooking.

LENTILS
Lentil go well with beans and are superb in soups and casseroles and as the basis for a hearty salad. They mix well with a huge range of different ingredients,

PREPARING DRIED PULSES

All pulses contain a toxin called lectin. Soaking and cooking are essential to render it harmless. To long-soak, place in a large bowl and cover with four times the volume in cold water. Soya beans and chickpeas may need to soak for eight hours or overnight until they appear plump.. To quick soak, bring the beans to the boil in a saucepan containing four times their volume in water. Boil for 3-5 minutes then leave to stand for an hour.

COOKING TIMES FOR BEANS	LENGTH OF COOKING TIME MAY VARY ACCORDING TO QUANTITY SO THESE ARE GUIDELINES ONLY.
VARIETY	COOKING TIME
MUNG, FLAGEOLET	45-50 MINUTES
ADUKI, BLACK-EYE, BORLOTTI, CANNELLONI, PINTO	50-60 MINUTES
HARICOT	60-70 MINUTES
BLACK, BUTTER, LIMA, CHICKPEA, RED KIDNEY	60-90 MINUTES
SOYA	UP TO FOUR HOURS

nuts

both sweet and savoury. Lentils just need picking over and rinsing before cooking. For whole lentils, bring to the boil and cook until just soft. With split lentils, used for purées or sauces, measure the water exactly to avoid a gloopy mixture: 250g lentils to 500ml water is a useful guide.

NUTS AND SEEDS

To add extra flavour, texture and nutritional value to a wide range of dishes, add some nuts. They contain healthy polyunsaturated fats as well as iron, zinc and magnesium. Roasting or grilling nuts and seeds enhances their flavour. Spread in a shallow baking sheet and cook in the oven at 200°C, gas mark 6 for 6-10 minutes.

PISTACHIO
Delicious in savoury grain dishes and salads and in ice cream where the slight almond flavour will be to the fore.

WALNUT
The strong flavour makes walnuts a good base for roasts and burgers. They are good in salads and with grains as well as adding crunch to cakes and breads.

PINE NUT
Serve lightly toasted in salads or with roasted vegetables. They work well with tomatoes and peppers and are a key ingredient of pesto sauces.

CASHEW
Mild but distinctive, cashews are good with rice and stir-fries and with aromatic spices.

CHESTNUT
Low in fat compared to other nuts they are useful in roasts and bakes. Their slightly sweet flavour can be seasoned with herbs or soy sauce. When soaking dried chestnuts, keep the leftover stock to use as a base for soups.

SEEDS
Sunflower, sesame and pumpkin seeds add texture and flavour to salads, breads and dressings. All can be toasted or eaten raw.

brea

fast
and brunch

BREAKFAST AND BRUNCH

SWEETCORN GRIDDLECAKES WITH YOGHURT SAUCE

These griddlecakes make a delicious Sunday breakfast treat; they are also good as a light lunch with a crispy green salad or served as a side dish with a main meal.

75g cornmeal
75g strong white flour
2 teaspoons baking powder
Salt and black pepper
1 tablespoon vegetable oil, plus extra for greasing the pan
150ml skimmed milk or water
1 cob fresh sweetcorn, or 125g canned sweetcorn, or frozen sweetcorn, defrosted
2 tablespoons chopped fresh coriander
2 egg whites

FOR THE SAUCE
150g low-fat Greek yoghurt
Grated zest of 1 lemon
1 tablespoon lemon juice
2 tablespoons chopped fresh coriander

PREPARATION TIME 5 minutes, plus 20 minutes standing
COOKING TIME 20 minutes
MAKES 12

1 Combine the cornmeal, flour, baking powder and some black pepper in a large bowl. Add the oil and the milk or water, and stir until the batter has a thick, dropping consistency. **2** If using fresh sweetcorn, cut off the tip and stand the cob upright on a chopping board. Hold it firmly by the stem and, using a sharp knife, slice off the kernels, following the hard cob as your guide. Add the sweetcorn kernels and chopped coriander to the batter, mix well, cover and allow to rest for 20 minutes. **3** Whisk the egg whites and a pinch of salt into soft peaks. Add a little beaten white to the batter to loosen it, then fold in the rest. **4** Heat a griddle or large frying pan and spread a thin coating of oil over it with a piece of kitchen paper. Keep the paper to hand and use it to grease the pan for the next batch. **5** Dip a large tablespoon in water and use it to drop spoonfuls of the batter onto the hot griddle or pan. Cook for 2–3 minutes until browned, then turn them over and cook for a further 3–4 minutes. Keep the first batch warm and repeat until all the batter has been used, greasing the griddle or pan after each batch. **6** To make the sauce, mix all the ingredients in a bowl and serve with the griddlecakes.

NUTRIENTS PER SERVING KCAL 760 • CARBOHYDRATE 12g (of which 1g sugars) • PROTEIN 3g • FAT 2g (of which saturated fat 0.1g) • FIBRE 0.5g • SODIUM 114mg • SALT 0.2g • VEGETABLE PORTION 0

BAKED MIXED MUSHROOMS WITH CIABATTA

A mix of olive oil, garlic and rosemary releases a wonderful Mediterranean aroma while the mushrooms are cooking. Served on crusty slices of hot ciabatta, the result is irresistible.

3 cloves garlic, crushed
2 teaspoons lemon juice
2 tablespoons olive oil
2 teaspoons balsamic vinegar
Salt and black pepper
675g mixed button, chestnut and open mushrooms
300g tomatoes
2-4 sprigs of rosemary
1 teaspoon chopped fresh parsley or sage
1 ciabatta loaf

PREPARATION TIME 15 minutes
COOKING TIME 20–25 minutes
SERVES 4 as a snack, or 8 as a starter

1 Heat the oven to 200°C (400°F, gas mark 6). Whisk together the garlic, lemon juice, olive oil, vinegar and seasoning in a large bowl. **2** Clean and slice the mushrooms; peel, deseed and dice the tomatoes. Add both to the bowl of dressing. Chop the rosemary, reserving some for a garnish, then add it to the mushroom mixture with the parsley or sage and stir. **3** Tip the mushroom mixture into a roasting tin. Cover with foil, make slits in the top to release a little of the steam during cooking and bake for 20–25 minutes, until the mushrooms are tender. **4** When they are nearly done, heat the bread in the oven. Cut it in half lengthways and cut each half into four equal pieces, or eight if serving as a starter. **5** Place two pieces of bread on each serving plate, cut side up, top with the mushroom mixture and serve immediately, garnished with the reserved rosemary.

NUTRIENTS PER SERVING KCAL 254 • CARBOHYDRATE 34g (of which 6g sugars) • PROTEIN 9g • FAT 9g (of which saturated fat 2g) • FIBRE 4g • SODIUM 351mg • SALT 0.8g • VEGETABLE PORTION 3

GRILLED VEGETABLE BRUSCHETTA

Grilling brings out all the sweet flavours of an assortment of Mediterranean vegetables.
Pile them on top of crusty bread that has been rubbed with garlic and tomato for extra zest.

1 medium red pepper
1 medium yellow pepper
2 small courgettes
1 medium head fennel
1 red onion
5 tablespoons olive oil
2 cloves garlic
1 small tomato
1 ciabatta loaf or 1 baguette
Salt and black pepper
6 large basil leaves

TOTAL TIME 30 minutes
SERVES 4

1 Preheat the grill to high. Rinse and dry the peppers, courgettes and fennel. Cut the peppers lengthways into eight, then remove their stems and any seeds. Trim the courgettes and slice them diagonally. Trim the fennel, then cut it lengthways into thin slices. Peel the onion and slice it into rings. **2** Cover the grill rack with tin foil and put a single layer of vegetables on it, laying the peppers skin-side down. Brush with olive oil and grill, on one side only, until they are lightly browned but still slightly firm. If necessary, cook them in batches and keep the first batch warm in the oven. **3** Meanwhile, peel and halve the cloves of garlic and rinse, dry and halve the tomato. Cut the loaf lengthways and then across into quarters and toast on both sides. **4** Rub the top of each slice with the cut garlic and tomato, then pile the grilled vegetables on top. Trickle over the remaining oil and season the bruschetta to taste. Rinse, dry and tear the basil leaves and scatter them over the top.

NUTRIENTS PER SERVING KCAL 338 • CARBOHYDRATE 40g (of which 9g sugars) • PROTEIN 9g
• FAT 16g (of which saturated fat 2g) • FIBRE 4g • SODIUM 343mg • SALT 0.9g
• VEGETABLE PORTION 2

APPLE AND CHEESE GRILLS

Cut thick slices from a large loaf of good wholemeal bread for this fruity version of cheese on toast, where a sweet layer of dessert apple lies hidden beneath the golden topping.

2 small red dessert apples
4 thick slices wholemeal bread
150g Cheddar, Cheshire or Emmental cheese
Butter for spreading
8 sage leaves
Black pepper

TOTAL TIME 15 minutes
MAKES 4

1 Preheat the grill to the highest setting. Rinse the apples, then quarter, core and slice them finely. **2** Toast the bread on one side under the grill. Meanwhile, finely slice or grate the cheese. **3** Turn the bread over and spread the untoasted side with butter. Arrange the apple slices on top and cover with cheese. Grill for 4 – 5 minutes, until the cheese melts and the apples heat through. **4** Meanwhile, rinse, dry and finely chop the sage leaves. When the grills are ready, sprinkle them with the chopped sage and black pepper and serve immediately.

NUTRIENTS PER SERVING KCAL 327 • CARBOHYDRATE 26g (of which 8g sugars) • PROTEIN 14g • FAT 18g (of which saturated fat 11g) • FIBRE 3.5g • SODIUM 545mg • SALT 1.3g • VEGETABLE PORTION 0

Apples are a good source of vitamin C, which is an antioxidant and helps to maintain the immune system.

GLAMORGAN SAUSAGES

Instead of meat, Glamorgan sausages are made with cheese, which, as the Welsh name suggests, should be Caerphilly. Celery has been added to lighten the texture and add a little crunch.

2 thin celery sticks, white part only, very finely chopped
175g fresh wholemeal breadcrumbs
115g Caerphilly cheese, finely grated
1 tablespoon chopped parsley
Black pepper
1 large egg, beaten
About 2 tablespoons milk
Plain flour for shaping
Olive oil for brushing

FOR THE WATERCRESS SAUCE
70g watercress
175g low-fat fromage frais
Salt and black pepper

PREPARATION TIME 10 minutes
COOKING TIME 5 minutes
SERVES 4

1 For the watercress sauce, bring a saucepan of water to the boil, add the watercress and return to the boil. Drain at once, pressing out excess moisture with the back of a spoon. Chop finely, then put in a bowl. Add the fromage frais and mix well. Add salt and pepper to taste and set aside. **2** Put the celery, breadcrumbs, cheese and parsley in a bowl, add black pepper and stir to mix. Using a fork, quickly mix in the egg and just enough milk to bind the mixture. **3** Divide the mixture into eight. Using floured hands, lightly roll each piece into a sausage shape about 10cm long. **4** Heat the grill and lightly brush the sausages with oil. Grill the sausages for about 5 minutes until golden, turning them occasionally. Serve with the watercress sauce and a leafy salad.

NUTRIENTS PER SERVING KCAL 320 • CARBOHYDRATE 21g (of which 3g sugars) • PROTEIN 17g • FAT 20g (of which saturated fat 10g) • FIBRE 3g • SODIUM 412mg • SALT 1g • VEGETABLE PORTION 0

CRUSHED BEANS ON TOAST

A sophisticated, fresh-flavoured version of the canned snack, using butter beans instead of the navy beans used in commercial recipes – an excellent source of protein, minerals and fibre.

4 cloves garlic
5 tablespoons olive oil
Handful of flat-leaved parsley
Salt and black pepper
400g canned butter beans, drained and rinsed
1 small onion, finely chopped
1 bay leaf
2–3 teaspoons fresh thyme leaves
2 slices of bread, tomato flavoured (optional), toasted

PREPARATION TIME 5 minutes
COOKING TIME 10 minutes
SERVES 2

1 Put the garlic into a small saucepan, cover with water and simmer for 5 minutes. Drain and put into a blender with 4 tablespoons of the oil and the parsley. Blend to a purée, add salt and pepper to taste and set aside. **2** Meanwhile, heat the remaining oil in a saucepan. Add the beans, onion, bay leaf and thyme and cook for 2-3 minutes, crushing the beans coarsely with a fork, until warmed through. Discard the bay leaf. **3** Add salt and pepper to taste and pile the beans onto the toast. Top with the parsley sauce and serve.

NUTRIENTS PER SERVING KCAL 500 • CARBOHYDRATE 47g (of which 6g sugars) • PROTEIN 15g • FAT 29g (of which saturated fat 4g) • FIBRE 10g • SODIUM 1023mg • SALT 2.6g • VEGETABLE PORTION 1

SPICY SCRAMBLED EGGS ON TOAST

Scrambled eggs become a tasty treat when cooked with fresh herbs, spices and a splash of lime juice. A far cry from bland nursery food, this dish holds its own as a late-night snack, too.

4 thick slices wholemeal bread
1 tablespoon butter
1 green chilli, deseeded and diced
2 teaspoons curry paste
1 clove garlic, crushed
1 teaspoon grated ginger
4 spring onions, chopped
85g tomatoes, peeled and diced
6 eggs
1 tablespoon chopped fresh coriander
1 teaspoon lime juice
Salt and black pepper
4 tablespoons low-fat natural yoghurt, optional

PREPARATION TIME 15 minutes
COOKING TIME 8–10 minutes
SERVES 4

1 Toast the bread and keep it warm. **2** Melt the butter in a nonstick frying pan and add the chilli, curry paste, garlic, ginger and spring onions, reserving a few for a garnish. Fry them over a low heat for 5 minutes, until softened but not browned. Stir in the tomatoes and cook for a further minute. **3** Beat the eggs with the coriander, lime juice and salt and pepper to taste. Add the eggs to the pan and stir gently over a low heat until just set. **4** Lay the toast on plates, top with the curried eggs, sprinkle with the reserved spring onions and add some yoghurt if you wish.

NUTRIENTS PER SERVING KCAL 272 • CARBOHYDRATE 17g (of which 4g sugars) • PROTEIN 17g • FAT 16g (of which saturated fat 5g) • FIBRE 2g • SODIUM 399mg • SALT 1g • VEGETABLE PORTION 0

EGG WHITE OMELETTE WITH ASPARAGUS

The delicate flavour of asparagus replaces the taste of egg yolk in this feather-light, low-calorie, low-cholesterol omelette. If asparagus is out of season, use baby spinach or brocoli instead.

100g asparagus, trimmed, or asparagus tips
Salt and black pepper
4 egg whites
½ teaspoon sunflower oil

PREPARATION TIME 10 minutes
COOKING TIME 16 minutes
SERVES 1

1 Put a steamer on to boil, then steam the asparagus for 8 minutes, or until tender, and drain. Season to taste while still warm. **2** Whisk the egg whites until frothy but not forming peaks: the mixture should be pourable. Do not add salt as it will break down the froth. **3** Heat the oil in a small nonstick omelette pan or frying pan, swirling it around until it covers the bottom with a thin film. Pour in the omelette mixture and cook over a low to medium heat for 2–3 minutes, until the bottom is firm. **4** Slide the omelette onto a plate. Lay the asparagus in the pan, then carefully invert the omelette on top. Cook for another 2–3 minutes, until the bottom has just set and the asparagus is golden brown, then serve.

NUTRIENTS PER SERVING KCAL 89 • CARBOHYDRATE 2g (of which 2g sugars) • PROTEIN 14g • FAT 3g (of which saturated fat 0.5g) • FIBRE 1.5g • SODIUM 244mg • SALT 0.6g • VEGETABLE PORTION 1

snacks and

Starters

SNACKS AND STARTERS

AVOCADO AND WATERCRESS CREAM

A blend of creamy avocado and hot watercress, this pretty purée can be eaten with a teaspoon or served as a dip. Watercress is is an excellent source of vitamins C and E – and it tastes great, too.

A bunch of watercress
A few sprigs of parsley
A few spring onions
1 clove garlic
1 lemon
A few basil leaves
4 tablespoons olive oil

2 large avocados
Salt and black pepper
1 tablespoon green peppercorns in brine

TOTAL TIME 18 minutes
SERVES 4

1 Discard the stalks from the watercress, then rinse and dry the leaves. Rinse and dry the parsley and strip the leaves from the stems. **2** Rinse the spring onions, chop the green tops, leaving the whites for another dish, and put them into a blender or food processor with the parsley and watercress. **3** Peel the garlic and crush it into the parsley and watercress. Wash any wax from the lemon, grate the rind, squeeze out the juice and add both to the blender or processor. Rinse and dry the basil leaves, then chop a few and set them aside for a garnish. Add the remaining leaves to the mixture with the olive oil. **4** Halve and stone the avocados. Leaving the shells intact, spoon the flesh into the blender or processor and season. Process until smooth. **5** Spoon the purée into the shells, sprinkle it with the peppercorns and reserved basil and serve. For a variation, garnish the plate with frisée lettuce and serve with Melba toast.

NUTRIENTS PER SERVING KCAL 300 • CARBOHYDRATE 2.5g (of which 1g sugars) • PROTEIN 3g • FAT 30g (of which saturated fat 6g) • FIBRE 4g • SODIUM 19mg • SALT trace • VEGETABLE PORTION 1

The flesh of a ripe **avocado** is as good for you as it tastes.

AUBERGINE PÂTÉ

Warm aubergine pâté packed with herbs and spices makes a fine smoky-flavoured dish to start a meal or serve as a snack. Served hot or cold, it tastes wonderful and can be made in advance.

2 tablespoons olive oil
1 medium onion
1 large, firm aubergine
10 sun-dried tomatoes
6 small gherkins
3 cloves garlic
A few sprigs of fresh thyme
A few sprigs of fresh parsley

1 teaspoon wholegrain mustard
1 teaspoon balsamic vinegar
2 teaspoons capers
1 loaf of French bread
Salt and black pepper

TOTAL TIME 30 minutes
SERVES 4

1 Heat the oil gently in a frying pan. Peel the onion, chop it finely and fry for 5 minutes, or until soft. **2** Rinse the aubergine and cut it into 1cm cubes. Add them to the onion and stir over a moderate heat for 8–10 minutes, or until they have softened. **3** Drain and chop the sun-dried tomatoes and the gherkins and add them to the aubergines. Peel the garlic cloves and crush them in. **4** Rinse and dry the thyme and parsley. Strip off the leaves and chop finely. Reserve some parsley for a garnish and add the rest of the herbs to the pan, with the mustard, vinegar and capers. Simmer, stirring frequently, for 5 minutes. **5** Meanwhile, cut and toast the French bread, or dry fry it on a ridged griddle. **6** Season the aubergine mixture, then blend it in a food processor or mash it to a paste by hand. **7** Spoon the pâté onto individual plates, sprinkle with the reserved parsley and serve with the toast.

NUTRIENTS PER SERVING KCAL 357 • CARBOHYDRATE 55g (of which 8g sugars) • PROTEIN 10g • FAT 12g (of which saturated fat 1g) • FIBRE 4g • SODIUM 694mg • SALT 1.7g • VEGETABLE PORTION 1

CHEESE AND MUSHROOM PÂTÉ

This is a very good way of using up scraps of leftover vegetarian cheese, as well as making a healthy, satisfying snack or lunch. Mushrooms add a wonderful flavour and texture to the dish.

15g unsalted butter
5 large, flat mushrooms, about 225g, roughly chopped
1 large leek, trimmed and finely chopped
5 tablespoons half-fat crème fraîche
1 teaspoon English mustard
Pinch of freshly grated nutmeg

Ground black pepper
125g Cheddar or Lancashire cheese, crumbled

PREPARATION TIME 10 minutes, plus 1 hour chilling
COOKING TIME 10 minutes
SERVES 4

1 Melt the butter in a large saucepan. Add the mushrooms and leek, cover and cook over a medium heat for 5 minutes, stirring occasionally. Add the crème fraîche, mustard, nutmeg and some black pepper and cook, uncovered, for 5 minutes, until almost all the liquid has evaporated.
2 Transfer the mixture to a blender or food processor, add the cheese, and purée in short bursts until smooth. **3** Scrape the mixture into a bowl or four individual ramekin dishes and chill for at least 1 hour or overnight before serving with oatcakes and mixed crudités.

NUTRIENTS PER SERVING KCAL 200 • CARBOHYDRATE 2g (of which 1g sugars) • PROTEIN 10g • FAT 16g (of which saturated fat 11g) • FIBRE 1g • SODIUM 236mg • SALT 0.6g • VEGETABLE PORTION 0

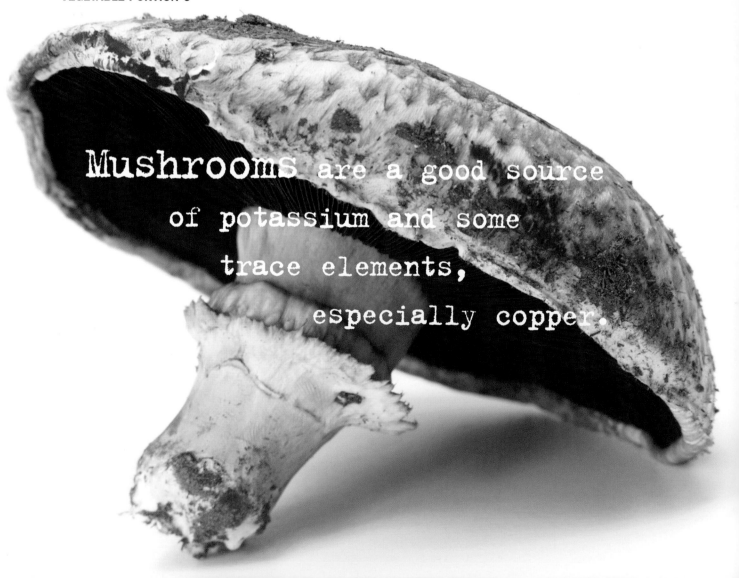

Mushrooms are a good source of potassium and some trace elements, especially copper.

BRANDIED CHESTNUT AND MUSHROOM TERRINE

The chestnuts in this flavour-packed dish contain only a fraction of the fat in most other nuts.

1 tablespoon olive oil, plus extra for greasing
2–4 cloves garlic, crushed
175g mushrooms, sliced
175g red onions, thinly sliced
6 tablespoons brandy
8 vacuum packed or canned unsweetened, whole chestnuts
1 egg, beaten
125g wholemeal breadcrumbs
400g canned unsweetened chestnut purée
Grated zest of ½ orange plus juice of 1 orange

1 tablespoon each chopped fresh parsley and thyme
Salt and black pepper

TO GARNISH chopped fresh coriander or basil
TO SERVE mixed salad leaves

PREPARATION TIME 20 minutes
COOKING TIME 55 minutes
SERVES 8–10

1 Heat the oven to 180°C (350°F, gas mark 4). Lightly grease a 900g loaf tin. 2 Heat the oil in a large saucepan over a medium heat and gently fry the garlic, mushrooms and onions for 7–8 minutes until they are tender and lightly browned, stirring frequently. 3 Add the brandy to the pan and allow it to simmer for 1–2 minutes until reduced, then remove the pan from the heat and leave the mixture to cool for about 3 minutes. 4 Break the chestnuts into pieces and stir them into the mushroom mixture with the egg, breadcrumbs, chestnut purée, orange zest and juice, parsley, thyme and salt and pepper to taste, using a wooden spoon to break up the chestnut purée. 5 When the mixture is thoroughly combined, spoon it into the loaf tin, smooth over the top and bake it for 45 minutes, or until the top is browned. 6 Leave the terrine to cool in the tin, then turn it out onto a plate and cut it into neat slices. Sprinkle a little chopped coriander or basil over the top and serve it with mixed salad leaves.

NUTRIENTS PER SERVING KCAL 234 • CARBOHYDRATE 38g (of which 6g sugars) • PROTEIN 6g
• FAT 4g (of which saturated fat 1g) • FIBRE 4g • SODIUM 97mg • SALT 0.2g
• VEGETABLE PORTION 0

GARLICKY FLAGEOLET BEAN TERRINE

Wrapped in shining green vine leaves and studded with stuffed green olives, this creamy terrine is a real winner. Serve it with crisp chicory leaves, fresh orange segments and crusty French bread for an unusual and attractive starter.

225g dried flageolet beans, soaked for at least 8 hours
1 small onion, halved
strip of lemon zest
2 bay leaves
10 vine leaves preserved in brine, or as needed
115g curd cheese
2 garlic cloves, crushed
1tbsp lemon juice
2 eggs, lightly beaten
2tbsp chopped parsley
50g pimiento-stuffed green olives, sliced
salt and pepper

TO SERVE 1 small head chicory, leaves separated
2 oranges, peeled and segmented
45g toasted almonds

PREPARATION AND COOKING TIME 2¾ hours, plus 6–8 hours soaking and 2 hours chilling
SERVES 8

1 Drain the soaked beans and rinse under cold running water. Put them in a saucepan with the onion, lemon zest, bay leaves and enough cold water to cover generously. Bring to the boil and boil rapidly for 10 minutes, then reduce the heat and simmer for 45–60 minutes or until tender. **2** Meanwhile, drain the vine leaves and rinse them in cold water. Spread out on kitchen paper and pat dry. Lightly oil a 900g terrine dish or loaf tin and line it with the vine leaves, shiny side out, allowing them to hang over the top of the dish. Set aside. **3** Preheat the oven to 180°C (350°F, gas mark 4). Drain the beans and discard the onion, lemon zest and bay leaves. Tip the beans into a bowl and mash with a potato masher until fairly smooth. **4** Add the curd cheese, garlic, lemon juice, eggs, parsley, and salt and pepper to taste. Mix together, then fold in the olives. Spoon into the prepared terrine dish or tin, pressing the mixture into the corners. Level the top, then fold over the overhanging leaves. Cover with additional leaves, if necessary. **5** Cover the top of the dish or tin with a piece of oiled foil, tucking the edges under the rim to seal securely. Set the dish in a roasting tin and pour enough warm water into the tin to come two-thirds of the way up the sides of the dish. Bake for 1 hour or until the top of the terrine feels firm to the touch. Remove the dish from the water, set it on a wire rack and leave to cool. Chill for at least 2 hours before serving. **6** To unmould, run a knife round the edges of the terrine and turn out onto a plate or board. Cut into slices and transfer to plates. Garnish each portion with chicory leaves, orange segments and almonds, and serve.

NUTRIENTS PER SERVING KCAL 177 • CARBOHYDRATE 15g (of which 6g sugars) • PROTEIN 13g • FAT 8g (of which saturated fat 2g) • FIBRE 9g • SODIUM 203mg • SALT 0.5g • VEGETABLE PORTION 0

FRESH HERB DIP WITH CHICKPEA CRÊPES

A feast of summery herbs is packed into this lemon-flavoured dip, served with tasty little pancakes.

FOR THE HERB DIP
A few sprigs each of basil, chives, dill and/or parsley
200ml crème fraîche
½ lemon
1 small clove garlic
Salt and black pepper

FOR THE CRÊPES
115g gram (chickpea) flour
115g plain flour
2 tablespoons olive oil
400ml lukewarm water

TOTAL TIME 30 minutes
SERVES 4

1 To make the herb dip, rinse, dry and finely chop enough herbs to give 4 tablespoons. Put the herbs into a small bowl with the crème fraîche and 1 tablespoon of lemon juice. Peel the garlic and crush it into the dip, mix well and add salt and pepper to taste. **2** To make the crêpes, put the gram and plain flour into a bowl. Add the oil and water gradually, whisking until the batter is smooth. Transfer to a measuring jug. **3** Heat a 15cm nonstick frying pan over a high heat, then pour in just under 50ml of the batter, tilting the pan so it covers the base evenly. Cook the crêpe for 30 seconds or until it is golden, flip it over and cook the other side for about 15 seconds. **4** Turn the crêpe onto a plate and roll it up. Keep it warm while you cook and roll the rest of the crêpes, then cut them in half and serve them with the dip.

NUTRIENTS PER SERVING KCAL 429 • CARBOHYDRATE 38g (of which 3g sugars) • PROTEIN 10g • FAT 27g (of which saturated fat 14g) • FIBRE 4g • SODIUM 23mg • SALT trace • VEGETABLE PORTION 0

Garlic and other members of the onion family may help to lower blood pressure and blood cholesterol.

Eggs are an excellent source of vitamin B_{12}, which is vital for the healthy functioning of the nervous system.

CROWDIE EGGS

Crowdie is a Scottish fresh cheese, traditionally made by crofters. The name comes from the Lowland Scots word 'cruds', meaning curds.

1.2 litres skimmed milk
Juice of ½ lemon
Salt and black pepper
3 large hard-boiled eggs, peeled and finely chopped
Grated zest of 1 unwaxed lemon
1 tablespoon each finely chopped chives and chervil

1 tablespoon low-fat mayonnaise
2 spring onions, finely chopped

PREPARATION TIME 10 minutes, plus cooling and chilling
COOKING TIME 12 minutes
SERVES 4

1 Put the milk in a jug and add the lemon juice. Leave to stand for 20–30 minutes, until soured. Transfer to a saucepan and place over a very low heat until just warm, but not simmering, and the liquid whey separates from the curds. Remove from the heat and leave to cool, then drain off the whey. **2** Line a colander with a clean tea towel. Pour in the curds and leave until most of the remaining whey has drained. Gather up the corners of the cloth and squeeze out the last of the liquid. Transfer to a bowl – there should be about 140g. Add a pinch of salt, beat until smooth and set aside. **3** Put the chopped egg in a bowl with the lemon zest, chives and chervil, mayonnaise and pepper. **4** Fold the eggs into the curds until mixed. Spoon into four ramekin dishes and sprinkle with the spring onions. Chill for 30 minutes, then serve with oatcakes.

NUTRIENTS PER SERVING KCAL 174 • CARBOHYDRATE 14g (of which 14g sugars) • PROTEIN 16g • FAT 7g (of which saturated fat 2g) • NO FIBRE • SODIUM 232mg • SALT 0.6g • VEGETABLE PORTION 0

ROASTED ASPARAGUS WITH CARAMELISED SHALLOT DRESSING

Roasting asparagus is a healthier alternative to drenching it in butter. For a smoky flavour, cook lightly oiled asparagus on the barbecue, turning the spears once or twice.

500g asparagus, trimmed
4 teaspoons olive oil
6 large cloves garlic
4 shallots
3 tablespoons balsamic vinegar
Salt and black pepper
1 tablespoon chopped fresh thyme, sage and
  rosemary mixed, or all thyme

PREPARATION TIME 10 minutes, plus 2-3 hours
  cooling, optional
COOKING TIME 20 minutes
SERVES 4

1 Heat the oven to 230°C (450°F, gas mark 8). **2** Place the asparagus in an ovenproof dish, drizzle with 2 teaspoons of the oil and use your fingers to rub it in so that all the spears are well coated. Roast the asparagus for 15–20 minutes, depending on the thickness of the spears, until they have softened and browned slightly. **3** Meanwhile, peel and quarter the garlic and shallots. Heat the rest of the oil in a wok or heavy-based pan, add the garlic and shallots and stir-fry over a high heat for 5–7 minutes until they are golden brown. **4** Add 4 tablespoons of water, reduce the heat, cover and simmer for 10–15 minutes until softened. Then increase the heat and boil hard until most of the water has evaporated. **5** Add the vinegar and bring to the boil, then pour the dressing over the hot asparagus. Season with salt and pepper to taste, and sprinkle with the herbs. Serve immediately, or set aside for a few hours to allow the flavours to mature, then serve at room temperature.

NUTRIENTS PER SERVING KCAL 76 • CARBOHYDRATE 6g (of which 6g sugars) • PROTEIN 4g • FAT 4g (of which saturated fat 0.5g) • FIBRE 2.5g • SODIUM 2mg • SALT trace • VEGETABLE PORTION 1

TURKISH AUBERGINE WITH TOMATO AND YOGHURT SAUCE

Flavoursome spoonfuls of yoghurt, tomato and toasted cumin seeds make a tasty partner for slices of smoky aubergine grilled with very little fat.

600g aubergines
2 tablespoons olive oil
2 teaspoons cumin seeds
100g canned chopped tomatoes
100g low-fat natural yoghurt
Salt and black pepper

TO GARNISH fresh coriander leaves

PREPARATION TIME 10 minutes
COOKING TIME 15 minutes, plus cooling
SERVES 4

1 Heat a ridged, cast-iron grill pan over a medium-high heat. Cut the aubergines widthways into 12 thick slices, discarding the ends. Lightly brush both sides of each slice with oil and cook for 3–4 minutes on each side until the flesh is soft when pierced. Alternatively, you can cook the aubergine slices under a hot grill. **2** Set the cooked aubergine slices aside to cool: they taste best at room temperature. **3** Meanwhile, heat a small frying pan over a high heat. Dry-fry the cumin seeds for a few seconds, or until they turn dark brown. Remove them from the pan immediately and set aside. When they are cool, grind them to a powder in a spice mill or with a pestle and mortar. **4** Put the tomatoes in a saucepan and cook over a medium heat for 3–4 minutes, stirring occasionally, until they are reduced to a thick sauce, then set this aside to cool. **5** When the tomato sauce has cooled, add the ground spice and yoghurt, mix together and season to taste. If you have time, chill the sauce a little. **6** To serve, lay three slices of the chargrilled aubergine on each of four plates and add a spoonful of the tomato and yoghurt sauce along the side of each. Garnish with a few fresh coriander leaves and serve.

NUTRIENTS PER SERVING KCAL 89 • **CARBOHYDRATE 6g (of which 2.5g sugars)** • **PROTEIN 3g**
• **FAT 6g (of which saturated fat 1g)** • **FIBRE 3g** • **SODIUM 29mg** • **SALT trace**
• **VEGETABLE PORTION 1**

WILD MUSHROOMS AND BLUEBERRIES ON RICE NOODLES

This stylish first course offers a rich and unusual contrast of tender mushrooms and refreshingly tart juicy fruit, tossed on a bed of mild rice noodles. For a variation, try using cranberries.

10g dried porcini mushrooms
150g baby chestnut mushrooms
150g oyster mushrooms
150g shiitake mushrooms
2 tablespoons olive oil
4 large cloves garlic, finely sliced
1 tablespoon finely sliced ginger
6 spring onions, sliced diagonally
350ml vegetable stock
2 tablespoons soy sauce
200g thin rice noodles
100g blueberries, defrosted if frozen

PREPARATION TIME 20 minutes, including soaking
COOKING TIME 30 minutes
SERVES 6

1 Rinse any grit off the porcini mushrooms, then leave them to soak in hot water for 20 minutes. Drain them, reserving the soaking liquid. Rinse, then dry them on kitchen paper and slice thinly. **2** Meanwhile, slice the baby chestnut and oyster mushrooms; remove and discard the stalks from the shiitakes then slice them. Set them all aside. **3** Heat the oil in a wok or a heavy-based frying pan. Add the garlic, ginger and spring onions and stir-fry for 4–5 minutes until the garlic is nicely browned. Add all the mushrooms and continue stir-frying for 2–3 minutes. **4** Make the reserved mushroom liquor up to 400ml with the stock and add it, with the soy sauce, to the mushrooms. Bring the mixture to the boil, then reduce the heat and simmer, uncovered, for 20 minutes, stirring occasionally. **5** Meanwhile, put a kettle of water on to boil. Put the rice noodles in a large heatproof bowl, cover them with the boiling water and leave them to soak for the time indicated on the packet. **6** Add the blueberries to the mushrooms, increase the heat and boil for 2–3 minutes until the liquid has thickened slightly and the blueberries are heated through. **7** Drain the noodles, add them to the mushroom mixture in the wok or frying pan and toss together. Spoon into six serving bowls and serve while still hot.

NUTRIENTS PER SERVING KCAL 177 • CARBOHYDRATE 30g (of which 3g sugars) • PROTEIN 4g • FAT 4g (of which saturated fat 1g) • FIBRE 1g • SODIUM 484mg • SALT 1.2g • VEGETABLE PORTION 0

Despite their misleading name, **sweet potatoes** are a healthy form of starch and a good source of potassium and vitamin C.

SPICED VEGETABLE WEDGES

For a really flavoursome dish choose a curry paste with a strong flavour.

About 700g mixed vegetables, such as celeriac, parsnips, sweet potatoes and squash, cut into chunks
4–5 tablespoons curry paste
Chopped coriander leaves to garnish

Low-fat Greek-style yoghurt to serve

PREPARATION TIME 10 minutes
COOKING TIME 25 minutes
SERVES 4

1 Heat the oven to 220°C (425°F, gas mark 7). Cook all the vegetables in boiling water: carrots and celeriac for 4–5 minutes, parsnips, sweet potatoes and squash for 3 minutes. Drain the vegetables well and put into a large bowl. **2** Stir the curry paste gently into the vegetables, until coated. **3** Spread the vegetables in a shallow baking dish and bake for about 20 minutes, or until tender. Stir once or twice during cooking to ensure even browning. **4** Sprinkle with coriander. Serve the wedges with a bowl of yoghurt, for dipping.

NUTRIENTS PER SERVING KCAL 140 • CARBOHYDRATE 21g (of which 7g sugars) • PROTEIN 3g • FAT 5g (of which saturated fat 1g) • FIBRE 6g • SODIUM 304mg • SALT 0.8g • VEGETABLE PORTION 2

INDIAN PATTIES

These spinach patties are usually deep-fried, but here they are grilled to give plenty of flavour with much less oil. Serve with a fruity chutney or a cooling raita.

225g split yellow lentils (channa dhal)
5cm cinnamon stick, broken into several pieces
4 cloves
2 teaspoons coriander seeds
2 teaspoons cumin seeds
½ teaspoon black peppercorns
2 teaspoons garlic purée, or crushed garlic
2 teaspoons ginger purée, or grated ginger
225g fresh spinach
2 tablespoons roughly chopped fresh coriander
8–10 fresh mint leaves, or ½ teaspoon dried mint
1–2 green chillies, deseeded
1 egg
Salt
50g onion, roughly chopped
1 tablespoon sunflower oil

TO GARNISH sprigs of fresh mint
TO SERVE 8 small pitta breads, grilled

PREPARATION TIME 25 minutes, plus 2–3 hours soaking
COOKING TIME 25 minutes
SERVES 8

1 Rinse the lentils, cover them with plenty of cold water and leave them to soak for 2–3 hours.
2 Heat a small, heavy-based frying pan over a medium heat. Add the cinnamon, cloves, coriander and cumin seeds and peppercorns, then dry-fry them for 1 minute, or until they release their aromas. Transfer them to a plate to prevent further cooking and leave to cool. **3** Drain the lentils and put them into a pan with the garlic, ginger and spinach. Cook over a medium heat, stirring, for 1–2 minutes until the spinach begins to release its juice. Reduce the heat, cover the pan and simmer for 10–12 minutes, stirring occasionally, until the liquid has been absorbed – take the lid off towards the end, if necessary, to allow it to evaporate. **4** Meanwhile, grind the roasted spices finely in a spice mill or with a pestle and mortar, then transfer them to a food processor. Add the lentil and spinach mixture, fresh coriander, mint, chilli, egg, and salt to taste and process. When the mixture is well blended, add the onion and pulse for a few seconds to chop the onion finely rather than puréeing it. **5** Heat the grill to high and divide the mixture into 16 equal balls. Shape them into round, flat patties about 5cm in diameter. **6** Line the grill pan with foil and brush lightly with some of the oil. Place the patties on top, brush them with half of the remaining oil and grill for 4 minutes. Turn them over, brush with the rest of the oil and grill for a further 3–4 minutes until brown and crisp. Serve two patties on a grilled pitta bread, garnished with a sprig of mint. As a variation, try using yellow split peas instead of the lentils.

NUTRIENTS PER SERVING KCAL 125 • CARBOHYDRATE 17g (of which 1g sugars) • PROTEIN 8g • FAT 3g (of which saturated fat 0.6g) • FIBRE 2.5g • SODIUM 61mg • SALT 0.15g • VEGETABLE PORTION 0

COURGETTE CAKES
WITH MINTED YOGHURT SAUCE

Chargrilled courgette cakes, served with a cool sauce, make a refreshing dish.

750g courgettes
Salt and black pepper
1 egg, beaten
60g matzo meal
A pinch of freshly grated nutmeg

FOR THE SAUCE
Finely grated zest and juice of ½ lemon
3–4 tablespoons chopped fresh mint
150g low-fat set yoghurt

TO GARNISH fresh sprigs of mint

PREPARATION TIME 15–30 minutes,
  plus 50 minutes standing
COOKING TIME 20 minutes
SERVES 4–6

1 Finely grate the courgettes into a colander, sprinkle with salt, mix well and allow to drain for 30 minutes. Rinse them under running water and squeeze dry with your hands, then place them in a clean tea towel and squeeze again. **2** Transfer the courgettes to a bowl and add the egg, matzo meal, nutmeg and pepper to taste. Mix them together until well combined, then allow to stand for 20 minutes for the flavours to develop. **3** To make the sauce, combine the lemon zest and juice, mint and yoghurt in a bowl, then cover and chill until ready to serve. **4** Heat a ridged, cast-iron grill pan or nonstick frying pan over a medium heat. Place dessertspoons of the courgette mixture onto the pan, flattening each to form a thick cake. Dry-fry the cakes for 4–5 minutes on each side, until they are firm and browned. (You may need to cook them in two batches.) Garnish with the mint and serve hot, with the chilled sauce on the side.

NUTRIENTS PER SERVING KCAL 129 • CARBOHYDRATE 18g (of which 6.5g sugars) • PROTEIN 8g • FAT 3g (of which saturated fat 1g) • FIBRE 2g • SODIUM 49mg • SALT 0.12g • VEGETABLE PORTION 2

WATERCRESS AND RICOTTA SOUFFLÉ

Watercress has been popular in Britain since the early 19th century. Grown beside streams, it has a robust and peppery taste which goes well with the mild, low-fat ricotta.

25g butter, plus extra for greasing
25g plain flour
300ml semi-skimmed milk
4 eggs, separated
115g ricotta cheese
25g mature vegetarian Cheddar cheese, grated

½ teaspoon English mustard
Salt and black pepper
85g watercress, trimmed and finely chopped

PREPARATION TIME 20 minutes
COOKING TIME 30 minutes
SERVES 6 as a starter

NUTRIENTS PER SERVING KCAL 180
- **CARBOHYDRATE 6g (of which 3g sugars)**
- **PROTEIN 10g**
- **FAT 12g (of which saturated fat 6g)**
- **NO FIBRE • SODIUM 160mg • SALT 0.4g**
- **VEGETABLE PORTION 0**

1 Heat the oven to 190°C (375°F, gas mark 5) and grease six 125ml ramekin dishes. **2** Melt the butter in a saucepan, stir in the flour and cook for 1 minute. Gradually stir in the milk to make a smooth sauce. Remove the pan from the heat, cool slightly, then stir in the egg yolks, one at a time. **3** Add the ricotta, Cheddar, mustard and salt and pepper to taste. Add the watercress, stirring well. In a clean bowl, whisk the egg whites until stiff. Beat 1 tablespoon of egg whites into the sauce, then fold in the remainder, using a metal spoon. **4** Spoon the mixture into the prepared dish and bake for 18–20 minutes or until risen and golden. Serve at once, with crusty bread and roasted tomatoes.

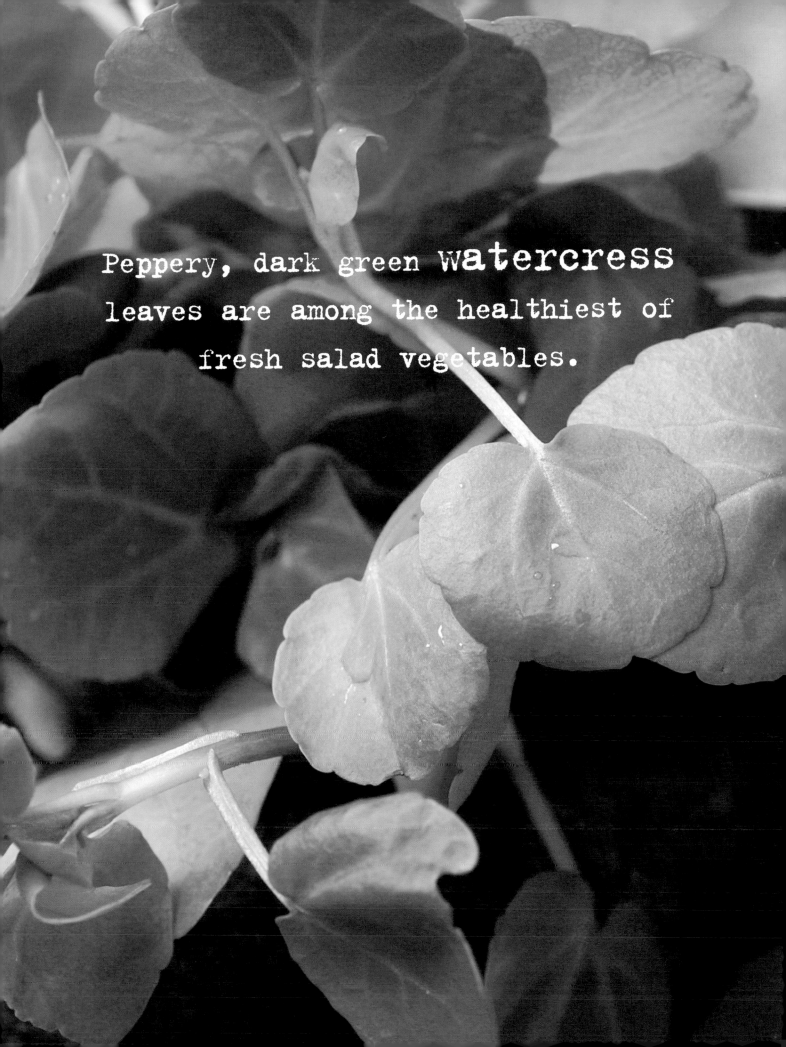

Peppery, dark green watercress leaves are among the healthiest of fresh salad vegetables.

Soups

SOUPS

GREEN BEAN SOUP

A trio of beans – green, broad and flageolet – fresh, frozen and canned, come together to add their individual flavours to this delicate, pale green soup, flavoured with chives.

2 tablespoons olive oil
1 litre vegetable stock
1 medium onion
1 large clove garlic
225g thin green beans
350g frozen broad beans
425g canned flageolet beans

Salt and black pepper

TO GARNISH a small bunch of chives

TOTAL TIME 30 minutes
SERVES 4–6

1 Heat the olive oil gently in a large saucepan and put the stock on to heat. Peel the onion, chop it and add it to the oil. Peel the garlic, crush it into the onion and stir. **2** Rinse, top and tail the green beans, chop into 2.5cm pieces and add them and the broad beans to the pan. Raise the heat and cook for a few minutes. **3** Add the stock to the pan and boil for 5 minutes, then lower the heat and simmer for 10 minutes. **4** Remove the saucepan from the heat and stir in the canned flageolet beans with their liquid. Stir well. **5** Process or blend half the soup to a purée, then return it to the pan. Season to taste, then reheat. Rinse the chives and any chive flowers, snip them over the soup and serve.

NUTRIENTS PER SERVING (4 portions) KCAL 185 • CARBOHYDRATE 20g (of which 5g sugars) • PROTEIN 11g • FAT 7g (of which saturated fat 1g) • FIBRE 10g • SODIUM 346mg • SALT 0.9g • VEGETABLE PORTION 2

Broad beans are nutritious, filling, inexpensive and can be enjoyed raw. They're a great low-fat, high-fibre food, and are full of minerals and vitamins

CREAMY AVOCADO AND COCONUT SOUP

Tropical flavours of chilli, coconut and coriander characterise this cold puréed soup, which takes its silky texture and velvety taste from luscious ripe avocados and smooth, creamy Greek yoghurt.

½ vegetable stock cube
4 spring onions
1 large clove garlic
1 fresh green chilli
A small bunch of coriander
2 medium avocados
300g natural Greek yoghurt
150ml coconut milk

1 tablespoon olive oil
A pinch of sugar
½ lemon
Salt and black pepper

TOTAL TIME 15 minutes
SERVES 4

1 Dissolve the stock cube in just a little hot water in a measuring jug, then make it up to 300ml with chilled water. 2 Rinse, trim and chop the spring onions. Peel and crush the garlic. Rinse, deseed and chop the chilli and set them all aside. 3 Rinse and dry the coriander. Set aside a few leaves for a garnish and roughly chop the remainder. 4 Halve and stone the avocados and scoop the flesh into a blender or food processor. Add the stock, spring onions, garlic, chilli, chopped coriander, yoghurt, coconut milk, olive oil, sugar and 1 tablespoon of juice from the lemon and process until velvety and smooth. 5 Season to taste and chill for as long as possible. Garnish with the coriander leaves and black pepper.

NUTRIENTS PER SERVING KCAL 342 • CARBOHYDRATE 8g (of which 5g sugars) • PROTEIN 7g
• FAT 31g (of which saturated fat 8g) • FIBRE 3g • SODIUM 202mg • SALT 0.5g
• VEGETABLE PORTION 1

HOT MOROCCAN BEAN SOUP

This filling soup is given extra heat with harissa, the fiery chilli paste from North Africa.

200g canned cannellini beans
400g canned chickpeas
150g onions, chopped
150g tomatoes, peeled and chopped
2 tablespoons lemon juice
1 teaspoon ground cumin
1 teaspoon turmeric
50g rice noodles
2 tablespoons chopped fresh coriander

1–2 teaspoons harissa paste
Salt and black pepper

TO GARNISH sprigs of fresh coriander

PREPARATION TIME 10 minutes
COOKING TIME 45 minutes
SERVES 4 as a main meal, or 6 as a starter

1 Rinse and drain the beans and chickpeas and place them in a large saucepan with the onions, tomatoes, lemon juice, cumin and turmeric. Add 1.7 litres of water. Bring to the boil, then reduce the heat, cover and simmer for 30 minutes. **2** Stir the rice noodles into the soup and simmer for a further 5 minutes. Then stir in the chopped coriander and the harissa and add salt and pepper to taste. **3** Ladle the soup into warmed bowls, garnish with sprigs of coriander and serve.

NUTRIENTS PER SERVING KCAL 200 • CARBOHYDRATE 35g (of which 5g sugars) • PROTEIN 10g • FAT 3g (of which saturated fat 0.5g) • FIBRE 7g • SODIUM 353mg • SALT 0.9g • VEGETABLE PORTION 2

BORSCHT WITH CORIANDER AND CUMIN

Beetroot is delicious teamed with other vegetables, as in this version of the Russian classic.

500g raw beetroot, chopped
1 stick celery, chopped
50g button mushrooms, sliced
150g onions, chopped
1 small red or yellow pepper, deseeded and chopped
175g potatoes, chopped
2 tablespoons olive or sunflower oil
2 teaspoons ground coriander
1 teaspoon cumin seeds

1.2 litres vegetable stock
A pinch of dried thyme
Salt and black pepper

TO GARNISH 150g low-fat natural yoghurt and chopped fresh chives

PREPARATION TIME 15 minutes
COOKING TIME 40 minutes
SERVES 6

1 Put the beetroot, celery, mushrooms, onions, pepper and potatoes into a large saucepan and stir in the oil. Cook over a high heat, stirring, until the vegetables start to sizzle. Cover the pan, reduce the heat to low and simmer for 10 minutes without lifting the lid. **2** Stir in the coriander and cumin and cook for a further 1–2 minutes. Add the stock and thyme, bring to the boil, then lower the heat and simmer for 20 minutes, stirring occasionally. **3** Season with salt and pepper to taste. Pour the soup into bowls and garnish each serving with yoghurt and a sprinkling of chives.

NUTRIENTS PER SERVING KCAL 115 • CARBOHYDRATE 16g (of which 10g sugars) • PROTEIN 4g
• FAT 5g (of which saturated fat 1g) • FIBRE 3g • SODIUM 274mg • SALT 0.7g
• VEGETABLE PORTION 2

BROCCOLI AND CAULIFLOWER CHEESE SOUP

A favourite family dish is transformed into a tasty, speckled soup, perfect for a light lunch or supper.

250g broccoli, broken into florets
250g cauliflower, broken into florets
1 shallot, or 50g onions, chopped
600ml vegetable stock
300ml skimmed milk
40g tiny pasta shapes for soup
75g half-fat mature Cheddar cheese, grated

1 tablespoon chopped fresh chives
Salt and black pepper

TO GARNISH a pinch of grated nutmeg

PREPARATION TIME 10 minutes
COOKING TIME 25 minutes
SERVES 4

1 Put the broccoli, cauliflower, shallot (or onions) and stock into a large saucepan. Bring to the boil, cover, then reduce the heat and simmer for 10 minutes, or until the florets are tender. Purée in a food processor or with a hand-held mixer. 2 Return the soup to the pan and add the milk and pasta. Gently bring it to a steady simmer, then cover and cook for a further 10 minutes, or until the pasta is tender. 3 Stir in the cheese and chives, reserving some chives for a garnish, and simmer for a few more minutes, stirring occasionally, until the cheese has melted and the soup has thickened slightly. Do not boil it or the cheese will become stringy. 4 Season to taste, garnish with the reserved chives and a sprinkling of nutmeg, and serve in warmed bowls.

NUTRIENTS PER SERVING KCAL 156 • CARBOHYDRATE 15g (of which 7g sugars) • PROTEIN 15g
• FAT 5g (of which saturated fat 2g) • FIBRE 3g • SODIUM 465mg • SALT 1.1g
• VEGETABLE PORTION 1

Unlike most other vegetables, **carrots** are more nutritious eaten cooked than raw. They are an excellent source of beta carotene, the plant form of vitamin A.

SPICY CARROT SOUP

Carrots and ginger bring out the best in each other. Here they are boosted with fresh green chilli and Eastern spices in a thick vegetable soup to make a real winter warmer.

1 litre vegetable stock or water
1 small to medium potato
1 medium onion
500g carrots
2 large cloves garlic
Salt and black pepper
1 fresh green chilli
5cm piece root ginger
1 lemon or lime

2 tablespoons olive oil
1 teaspoon garam masala, Chinese five-spice powder or mixed spice
1 teaspoon toasted sesame oil

TO GARNISH fresh coriander leaves, lemon or lime zest or croutons

TOTAL TIME 30 minutes
SERVES 4–6

1 Bring the stock or water to the boil in a large saucepan. Peel the potato, onion and carrots and cut them into small chunks. Peel and quarter the garlic cloves. **2** When the stock is boiling, stir in the vegetables, garlic and some salt. Bring it back to the boil, reduce the heat, partially cover and boil gently for 15–20 minutes. **3** Meanwhile, rinse, deseed and chop the chilli, peel and chop the ginger, and squeeze the juice from the lemon or lime. **4** Heat the olive oil in a small pan and fry the chilli and ginger for about 1 minute, but do not let them burn. Stir in the garam masala, five-spice powder or mixed spice and the juice; cook for 1 minute. **5** Add the sesame oil and stir over the heat until the mixture thickens to form a sauce. Remove the pan from the heat and set aside. **6** When the vegetables are tender, stir in the ginger sauce, then process or blend the mixture into a smooth purée. Return the purée to the pan, season with black pepper to taste, then reheat and serve with the garnish of your choice.

NUTRIENTS PER SERVING KCAL 149 • CARBOHYDRATE 19g (of which 9g sugars) • PROTEIN 3g • FAT 9g (of which saturated fat 1g) • FIBRE 4g • SODIUM 330mg • SALT 0.8g • VEGETABLE PORTION 1

COURGETTE AND WATERCRESS SOUP

The mellow smoothness of the courgettes in this intensely green vegetable soup provides a subtle counterbalance to the underlying sharp, peppery flavour of the watercress leaves.

2 medium onions
25g unsalted butter
700ml vegetable stock
900g firm courgettes
A large bunch of watercress

1 lemon
Salt and black pepper

TOTAL TIME 30 minutes
SERVES 4

1 Peel and chop the onions. Heat the unsalted butter in a large saucepan and fry the onions over a gentle heat until they are translucent. Add the stock, cover, and bring to the boil. **2** Rinse the courgettes, slice them thinly, and add them to the boiling stock. Reduce the heat, cover, and simmer for 15 minutes. **3** Rinse the watercress, discard the coarse stems and reserve four sprigs for a garnish. Chop the remainder. **4** When the courgettes are tender, stir in the watercress, then remove the pan from the heat and leave to stand, covered, for 5 minutes. Meanwhile, squeeze the juice from the lemon and set aside. **5** Blend the soup to a purée, add seasoning and lemon juice to taste. Reheat and garnish with watercress.

NUTRIENTS PER SERVING KCAL 119 • **CARBOHYDRATE 9g (of which 7g sugars)** • **PROTEIN 6g** • **FAT 6g (of which saturated fat 4g)** • **FIBRE 3g** • **SODIUM 302mg** • **SALT 0.76g** • **VEGETABLE PORTION 3**

COOL CUCUMBER SOUP

This is a great soup to make on a steamy summer's day since it requires no cooking at all. Just assemble the ingredients and mix them together, then it is ready to eat and enjoy.

1 large cucumber
4 bushy sprigs of mint
500g natural yoghurt
150ml single cream
2 tablespoons white wine vinegar
Salt and black pepper

TO GARNISH 4 small sprigs of mint
TO SERVE ice cubes, optional

TOTAL TIME 15 minutes
SERVES 4

1 Chill four soup bowls in the refrigerator. Trim, rinse and dry the cucumber then grate it coarsely, with its skin, into a large bowl. **2** Rinse and dry the bushy mint. Strip the leaves from the stalks and shred enough to give 4 tablespoons, or bundle the leaves together and cut them diagonally into fine strips with kitchen scissors. Add the mint to the cucumber. **3** Stir the yoghurt, cream and vinegar into the bowl. Season well with salt and pepper and stir again. **4** Divide the soup among the four chilled soup bowls. Add one or two ice cubes to each one, if you like, to chill it quickly. Garnish with the small sprigs of mint and serve.

NUTRIENTS PER SERVING KCAL 182 • CARBOHYDRATE 13g (of which 12g sugars) • PROTEIN 9g • FAT 11g (of which saturated fat 7g) • FIBRE 0.7g • SODIUM 114mg • SALT 0.3g • VEGETABLE PORTION 1

Fennel is a versatile vegetable; every part of it – leaves, stalks and bulb – can be used in cooking.

FENNEL, PEA AND MINT SOUP

An intensely coloured soup with just the right combination of smooth and chunky textures and herby flavours that sing through clearly, this makes a lovely light lunch, too.

600g fennel, chopped
500g fresh or frozen peas
900ml vegetable stock
3 tablespoons chopped fresh mint
Salt and black pepper

TO GARNISH a few small lettuce leaves, such as oak-leaf lettuce, and a few sprigs of fresh herbs, such as chervil and mint

PREPARATION TIME 5 minutes
COOKING TIME 25 minutes
SERVES 4–6

I Place the fennel, peas and stock in a large saucepan and bring to the boil, then reduce the heat, cover and simmer for 20 minutes, or until the fennel is tender. **2** Add the chopped mint and simmer for a further 1 minute. **3** Reserve a cupful of the vegetables and purée the remaining mixture in a food processor or with a hand-held mixer. Scrape the purée back into the pan. **4** Return the reserved vegetables to the soup and reheat. Season to taste with salt and pepper then serve, garnished with the lettuce leaves and herbs.

NUTRIENTS PER SERVING KCAL 127 • CARBOHYDRATE 18g (of which 5g sugars) • PROTEIN 10g • FAT 3g (no saturated fat) • FIBRE 9g • SODIUM 312mg • SALT 0.8g • VEGETABLE PORTION 3

MUSHROOM SOUP

The earthy flavour of the large, dark mushrooms in this soup is given a lift by garlic, parsley and mace. It has a deep, smoky colour and a rich taste that needs no cream to enhance it.

1.2 litres vegetable stock
140g rustic-style bread
½ small onion or 1 shallot
650g large, flat mushrooms
3 sprigs of parsley
2 tablespoons olive oil
½ small clove garlic
A pinch of ground mace or freshly grated
** nutmeg**
Salt and black pepper

TOTAL TIME 30 minutes
SERVES 4–6

1 Put the stock on to boil. Soak the bread in a little cold water. **2** Peel and chop the onion or shallot. Clean and roughly chop the mushrooms. Rinse, dry and chop the parsley. **3** Heat the oil in a large pan. Fry the onion or shallot over a moderate heat until lightly browned. Peel the garlic and crush it into the pan. Add the mushrooms and cook until they release their liquid; add the parsley. **4** Squeeze as much water as possible from the bread, then stir it into the mushrooms. Add the stock and mace or nutmeg. Return it to the boil, half cover the pan and simmer for 15–20 minutes. **5** Purée or blend the soup until it is creamy but still slightly grainy, then reheat, season with salt and pepper and serve.

NUTRIENTS PER SERVING KCAL 161 • CARBOHYDRATE 19g (of which 2g sugars) • PROTEIN 6g • FAT 7g (of which saturated fat 1g) • FIBRE 1.5g • SODIUM 400mg • SALT 1g • VEGETABLE PORTION 2

AROMATIC PARSNIP SOUP

This fragrant, warming winter soup has a yoghurt creaminess and subtle spicing, with a sweet undertone of apple. Serve it with hot, crusty bread for a hearty starter or light lunch.

850ml vegetable stock
1 large cooking apple
550g parsnips
1 medium onion
1 tablespoon sunflower oil
1 clove garlic
2 teaspoons ground coriander
1 teaspoon ground cumin
1 teaspoon turmeric
Salt
300ml milk

TO GARNISH a few sprigs of coriander;
  4–6 tablespoons natural yoghurt

TOTAL TIME 30 minutes
SERVES 4–6

1 Warm the stock over a low heat. Peel the apple and the parsnips. Quarter and core the apple, then chop the apple and parsnips into chunks and set aside. **2** Peel and chop the onion. Heat the oil in a large saucepan, add the onion and leave it to soften. **3** Peel and roughly chop the garlic, add it to the pan, then add the three spices and cook for 1 minute. **4** Pour the warmed stock into the pan and add the apple, parsnips and salt. Bring to the boil, then reduce the heat, cover and simmer for 15 minutes. **5** Meanwhile, rinse and dry the coriander and strip off the leaves. **6** Remove the pan from the heat and stir in the milk. Process or blend the soup to a smooth purée, then reheat. **7** Ladle the soup into bowls, garnish it with the coriander and serve. Prepare a dish of plain low fat yoghurt to hand around separately for people to help themselves.

NUTRIENTS PER SERVING KCAL 200 • CARBOHYDRATE 22g (of which 7g sugars) • PROTEIN 6g • FAT 8g (of which saturated fat 3g) • FIBRE 7g • SODIUM 345mg • SALT 0.9g • VEGETABLE PORTION 2

LEMONY LENTIL SOUP

This sturdy, soothing winter soup has a delicious citrus overtone combined with the warm flavours of roasted spices. It makes an interesting change from more familiar lentil-based soups.

1 tablespoon olive oil
3 cloves garlic, coarsely chopped
250g onions, coarsely chopped
250g red lentils, rinsed and drained
1.2 litres vegetable stock
1 teaspoon ground coriander
½ teaspoon ground cumin

Juice of 1 lemon
4 wafer-thin slices of lemon
Salt and black pepper

PREPARATION TIME 5 minutes
COOKING TIME 35 minutes
SERVES 4

1 Heat the oil in a heavy-based saucepan. Add the garlic and onions and cook them over a medium heat for 6–7 minutes until they turn a rich brown colour, stirring frequently to prevent them from sticking. **2** Add the lentils and cook for a further 1–2 minutes. Then add the stock, raise the heat and bring the soup to the boil. Reduce the heat, cover and simmer for 15–20 minutes until the lentils are almost soft. **3** Place a nonstick frying pan over a high heat, add the coriander and cumin and dry-fry them for 1–2 minutes until the aroma rises, then add them to the soup. **4** Raise the heat under the soup, add the lemon juice and lemon slices and season to taste, then let it simmer for 5 minutes. Sprinkle the soup with a little black pepper and serve.

NUTRIENTS PER SERVING KCAL 261 • **CARBOHYDRATE 40g (of which 5g sugars)** • **PROTEIN 18g** • **FAT 5g (of which saturated fat 1g)** • **FIBRE 4g** • **SODIUM 310mg** • **SALT 0.8g** • **VEGETABLE PORTION 1**

WINTER PUMPKIN AND RICE SOUP

This is a hearty, warming soup, perfect for cold, damp winter days. When puréed, the pumpkin and rice give the soup a velvety texture, and a little curry powder adds a subtle touch of heat. This soup makes a tempting and filling starter.

1kg pumpkin
2 tablespoons extra virgin olive oil
2 onions, chopped
1 teaspoon mild curry powder
2 garlic cloves, finely chopped
1 fresh, hot green chilli, seeded and finely chopped
1 litre vegetable stock
175g risotto rice
a little hot vegetable stock (optional)
1 tablespoon chopped fresh coriander
salt and pepper

PREPARATION TIME 20 minutes
COOKING TIME 40–45 minutes
SERVES 6

1 Peel the pumpkin and remove the seeds and fibres from the centre. Rinse the seeds and reserve. Cut the pumpkin flesh into cubes. **2** Heat the oil in a large saucepan, add the onions and curry powder, and cook over a low to moderate heat, stirring frequently, for 15–20 minutes or until the onions soften and start to caramelise. **3** Add the cubes of pumpkin, the garlic and chilli, and stir to coat with the onion mixture. Pour in the stock and add 5 tablespoons of the rice. Bring to the boil, then cover the pan, reduce the heat and simmer for 25 minutes or until the pumpkin and rice are very soft. **4** Meanwhile, bring a saucepan of water to the boil, add the remaining rice and simmer for about 15 minutes or until just tender. Drain in a sieve, rinse lightly under cold water and leave to drain again. **5** Preheat the grill to moderately high. Spread out the pumpkin seeds on a baking sheet in a single layer and toast under the grill for 3–5 minutes or until golden and aromatic, turning them several times. Set aside. **6** When the pumpkin and rice are soft, purée the soup, either in a blender or food processor, or using a hand-held blender directly in the pan.
7 Stir in the cooked rice and season with salt and pepper to taste. Reheat gently. If the soup seems too thick, stir in a little hot vegetable stock or water. Stir in the chopped coriander and serve, sprinkled with the toasted pumpkin seeds.

NUTRIENTS PER SERVING KCAL 179 • CARBOHYDRATE 30g (of which 6g sugars) • PROTEIN 4g • FAT 5g (of which saturated fat 1g) • FIBRE 2.5g • SODIUM 192mg • SALT 0.5g • VEGETABLE PORTION 3

RED PEPPER AND ORANGE VELVET SOUP

A soup to delight the senses, this derives its stunning colour from red peppers, and its heady aroma and fruity flavour from orange flower water and freshly squeezed orange juice.

2 tablespoons olive oil
1kg red peppers
Salt
3 oranges
1 tablespoon orange flower water

TO GARNISH orange zest, chopped parsley or croutons, optional

TOTAL TIME 30 minutes
SERVES 4

1 Heat the oil in a large saucepan over a moderate heat. Rinse, dry, deseed and quarter the peppers lengthways. Slice them fairly coarsely in a food processor and add to the oil. Alternatively, slice them by hand, adding the first pepper to the pan while you slice the next, stirring with each addition and keeping the pan covered while you slice. Add a little salt to taste. **2** Wash any wax from the oranges, then grate the rind from one into the pan. Cover, and increase the heat to high until steam starts to escape from under the lid. Lower the heat and simmer, covered, for 15–18 minutes, shaking the pan occasionally, allowing the peppers to cook in their own juice. **3** Meanwhile, squeeze the juice from the oranges into a measuring jug: you will need 175ml. Stir the orange flower water into the orange juice. **4** When the peppers are soft, process or blend them to a smooth purée. It does not matter if some of the peppers have caramelised – this just adds to the flavour. Add the orange mixture and process or blend again. **5** Reheat and garnish with orange zest, herbs and croutons, if using.

NUTRIENTS PER SERVING KCAL 130 • CARBOHYDRATE 17g (of which 16g sugars) • PROTEIN 2g • FAT 6g (of which saturated fat 1g) • FIBRE 4g • SODIUM 10mg • SALT trace • VEGETABLE PORTION 3

TOMATO AND BREAD SOUP

This variation on the traditional Italian peasant soup made with day-old bread gains a wonderful flavour from garlic, herbs and balsamic vinegar, and the bread gives it a satisfying texture,

2 tablespoons olive oil
150g onions, chopped
1 red chilli, deseeded and chopped
2 cloves garlic, crushed
1 tablespoon chopped fresh thyme
1kg tomatoes, cut into quarters
600ml vegetable stock
A pinch of sugar
125g day-old white bread, cubed
2 tablespoons balsamic vinegar

2 tablespoons chopped fresh basil leaves
Salt and black pepper

TO GARNISH fresh basil leaves

PREPARATION TIME 15 minutes, plus
** 10 minutes soaking time**
COOKING TIME 25 minutes
SERVES 6

1 Heat 1 tablespoon of the oil in a saucepan and fry the onions, chilli, garlic and thyme on a low heat for 5 minutes, or until they have softened and are lightly golden. **2** Add the tomatoes, stock and sugar to the onions and bring them to the boil. Cover the pan, reduce the heat and simmer for 20 minutes. **3** Meanwhile, put the bread cubes into a small bowl, add the vinegar, the remaining oil and 4 tablespoons of cold water and leave them to soak for 10 minutes. **4** Purée the tomato mixture, bread and basil together with a hand-held mixer or in a food processor until very smooth. **5** Return the soup to the pan, season to taste and reheat it gently. Pour the soup into warmed bowls, garnish with a few leaves of basil and serve.

NUTRIENTS PER SERVING KCAL 126 • CARBOHYDRATE 18g (of which 9g sugars) • PROTEIN 3g
• FAT 5g (of which saturated fat 1g) • FIBRE 2g • SODIUM 320mg • SALT 0.8g
• VEGETABLE PORTION 3

FRENCH VEGETABLE SOUP

This elegant combination of fresh spring vegetables, cooked together then added to a rich tomato-flavoured broth, makes a hearty soup that will serve as a main course for lunch or supper.

25g butter
2 cloves garlic
2 shallots
1.2kg canned chopped tomatoes
400ml vegetable stock
1 teaspoon dried sweet basil
Salt and black pepper
200g baby new potatoes
12 baby or 4 small carrots
6 large radishes
100g sugarsnap, or mangetout, peas
12 asparagus tips
125ml single cream
8 large basil leaves

TO GARNISH Mature Cheddar, optional

TOTAL TIME 30 minutes
SERVES 4

1 Put a kettle of water on to boil. Heat the butter very slowly in a large saucepan. Peel and chop the garlic and shallots, add them to the butter and fry gently for 3 minutes, stirring occasionally. **2** Add the tomatoes and their liquid, stock, dried basil, and some salt and pepper to the pan. Cover and simmer for 15 minutes. **3** Meanwhile, scrub and quarter the potatoes, put them into a second saucepan and cover well with the boiling water from the kettle. Bring back to the boil, then reduce the heat and boil gently. **4** Trim, scrub and halve the baby carrots or, if you are using larger ones, peel them and cut into 2.5cm chunks. When the potatoes have been cooking for about 5 minutes, add the carrots. **5** Trim and rinse the radishes, then dice them and add them to the carrots and potatoes. Rinse the asparagus tips and rinse, trim and halve the sugarsnap or mangetout peas and add them. **6** Cook the vegetables for a total of 10–12 minutes or until they are just tender. Meanwhile, grate the cheese, if using, and set aside. **7** Drain the vegetables and add to the tomato stock. Stir in the cream. Rinse, tear and add the basil leaves. **8** Season to taste with salt and pepper. Serve the soup immediately, ladling it into warmed bowls and passing round the grated cheese separately to sprinkle over the top, if you are using it.

NUTRIENTS PER SERVING KCAL 247 • CARBOHYDRATE 28g (of which 4g sugars) • PROTEIN 8g • FAT 12g (of which saturated fat 7g) • FIBRE 6g • SODIUM 488mg • SALT 1.2g • VEGETABLE PORTION 2

WINTER VEGETABLE SOUP

Other winter vegetables can also be used in this thick, warming soup. Try Jerusalem artichokes or swede in place of the parsnips or carrots. Accompany with garlic flavoured croutons.

1 tablespoon olive oil
25g butter
1 large onion, chopped
125g leeks, rinsed and sliced
280g parsnips, peeled and chopped
400g carrots, peeled and chopped
1 large potato, peeled and chopped
900ml vegetable stock

4–5 tablespoons semi-skimmed milk (optional)
Salt, black pepper and freshly grated nutmeg
2 tablespoons chopped parsley

PREPARATION TIME 20 minutes
COOKING TIME 35–40 minutes
SERVES 4

1 Heat the oil and butter in a large saucepan. Add the onion and leeks and cook, stirring, over a medium heat, for 4–5 minutes until soft. Add the parsnips, carrots and potato and cook, stirring, for 2–3 minutes. **2** Pour in the stock, bring to the boil, then simmer for 20–25 minutes until all the vegetables are tender. **3** Transfer to a blender or food processor and process until smooth. Return to the saucepan and pour in a little milk to thin, if needed. Season with salt, pepper and nutmeg, then stir in the parsley. **4** Reheat gently, then transfer to warmed bowls. Serve with bread or croutons that have been rolled in crushed garlic before grilling or frying.

NUTRIENTS PER SERVING KCAL 215 • CARBOHYDRATE 29g (of which 13g sugars) • PROTEIN 5g • FAT 9g (of which saturated fat 4g) • FIBRE 7g • SODIUM 377mg • SALT 0.9g • VEGETABLE PORTION 2

Few foods are more nourishing than milk. It is an important source of protein and contains essential calcium, B vitamins and zinc.

SPRING VEGETABLE SOUP WITH LEMON

This refreshing soup mixes unusual sour and sweet flavours. Serve it hot or chilled, with a glass of ice-cold vodka. Either way, it makes a delicious starter, full of the promise of summer.

125g potatoes, cut into cubes
150g onions, chopped
2 stalks lemongrass, tough outer leaves
 removed, finely chopped
1.2 litres vegetable stock
50g sorrel, finely shredded
50g spinach, finely shredded
50g spring onions, finely sliced
1 fresh red chilli, deseeded and finely chopped

2 cloves garlic, finely sliced
1–2 tablespoons sugar or clear honey
Salt
3–4 tablespoons lemon juice

PREPARATION TIME 15 minutes
COOKING TIME 20–25 minutes
SERVES 4

1 Place the potatoes, onions, chopped lemongrass and stock in a large heavy-based saucepan and bring it all to the boil. Reduce the heat, cover and simmer for 15–20 minutes until the potatoes are just cooked. **2** Stir in the sorrel, spinach, spring onions, chilli, garlic, sugar or honey and a pinch of salt. Bring the soup to the boil and cook for 1 minute. **3** Remove the soup from the heat and add lemon juice to taste. Serve it hot or chilled, as you prefer.

NUTRIENTS PER SERVING KCAL 59 • CARBOHYDRATE 10g (of which 7g sugars) • PROTEIN 4g • FAT 1g (no saturated fat) • FIBRE 2g • SODIUM 326mg • SALT 0.8g • VEGETABLE PORTION 0

GAZPACHO

This crunchy, floating salad, one of many versions of the celebrated Spanish soup, is incomparable on a hot day. The combination of textures and flavours is really satisfying.

1 thick slice dry-textured bread
6 tablespoons extra virgin olive oil
4 tablespoons red wine vinegar
Salt and black pepper
1 tablespoon paprika, or hot or sweet Spanish paprika (Pimenton)
600g canned chopped tomatoes in natural juice
1 red onion
4 large cloves garlic
1 large cucumber
1 each, medium red, yellow and green peppers
1 fresh or dried red chilli, or 1 fresh green chilli
6 large basil and/or mint leaves
300ml ice-cold water
12 ice cubes (if required)

TO GARNISH 1 clove garlic, a little olive oil and 3 slices of bread for croutons, optional

TIME 30 minutes
SERVES 4–6

1 Discard the crusts from the bread, then put it into a food processor and make it into crumbs. 2 Put the oil into a large serving bowl and whisk in the vinegar and salt to make a creamy emulsion. Add the paprika or Pimenton and the breadcrumbs and stir until thoroughly combined and sloppy. 3 Stir the tomatoes and their juice into the mixture then set it aside. 4 Peel the onion, garlic and cucumber. Rinse, halve and deseed the peppers and the chilli, then cut them into quarters. 5 In a food processor, coarsely chop the onion and garlic together and add them to the breadcrumb mixture. One by one, coarsely chop the cucumber, peppers and chilli and add them to the soup. 6 Rinse, dry and tear the basil or mint leaves into small pieces and add them. Stir well, taste and season generously with salt and black pepper. The flavour should be sharp and refreshing, with plenty of bite. 7 Stir in enough ice-cold water to give the mixture a soup-like consistency, but do not make it too thin: the texture should be quite dense. Leave to chill, or stir in the ice cubes and serve immediately. 8 To make croutons, put the garlic into a frying pan with a little oil, over a moderate heat. Cut the bread into cubes and fry, turning often, until browned. Discard the garlic; serve the croutons with the soup.

NUTRIENTS PER SERVING (4 portions) KCAL 261 • CARBOHYDRATE 21g (of which 13g sugars) • PROTEIN 6g • FAT 18g (of which saturated fat 3g) • FIBRE 3g • SODIUM 118mg • SALT 0.3g • VEGETABLE PORTION 4

VEGETABLE SOUP WITH FRAGRANT PESTO

This soup is based on pistou, the classic Provençale soup. Laden with vegetables and pasta and flavoured with pesto, it makes a fabulous change from minestrone, its Italian counterpart. French bread is the traditional accompaniment, plus a glass of wine.

1 tablespoon extra virgin olive oil
1 leek, thinly sliced
1 large courgette, diced
150g French beans, cut into short lengths
2 garlic cloves, crushed
1.3 litres vegetable stock
250g tomatoes, chopped
85g vermicelli, broken into small pieces

2 tablespoons pesto sauce
pepper

TO SERVE (optional) 4 tablespoons freshly grated Italian-style premium cheese

PREPARATION TIME 10 minutes
COOKING TIME about 30 minutes
SERVES 4

1 Heat the oil in a large saucepan. Add the leek, courgette, beans and garlic and fry over a moderately high heat for about 5 minutes or until the vegetables are softened and beginning to turn brown. **2** Pour in the vegetable stock. Stir in the tomatoes and add freshly ground black pepper to taste. Bring to the boil, then reduce the heat and cover the pan. Simmer over a low heat for 10 minutes or until the vegetables are tender, but still holding their shape. **3** Stir in the vermicelli. Cover the pan again and simmer for a further 5 minutes or until the pasta is al dente. **4** Ladle the soup into bowls and add 1½ teaspoons pesto to each. Stir, then serve, offering the grated cheese separately to stir into the soup.

NUTRIENTS PER SERVING KCAL 240 • CARBOHYDRATE 20.5g (of which 4g sugars) • PROTEIN 12g • FAT 12g (of which saturated fat 4.5g) • FIBRE 3g • SODIUM 416mg • SALT 1g • VEGETABLE PORTION 1

SALADS

TROPICAL SALAD WITH LIME DRESSING

Two favourite tropical fruits – rich, creamy-smooth avocado and sweet-flavoured papaya – are combined with watercress and a fresh lime dressing to make a light and stylish starter.

FOR THE SALAD
A bunch of watercress
2 ripe but firm avocados
2 ripe but firm papayas

FOR THE DRESSING
1 lime
Salt and black pepper
¼ teaspoon sugar
4 tablespoons extra virgin olive oil
4 tablespoons sunflower oil

TOTAL TIME 20 minutes
SERVES 4

1 First make the dressing. Wash any wax from the lime and remove the rind with a zester, or grate it finely. Squeeze out 2 tablespoons of lime juice and put it with the rind in a mixing bowl. Add salt, black pepper and the sugar, then whisk in the oils. Taste and add more lime juice, if necessary, then put the dressing aside. **2** Rinse and dry the watercress and trim off the coarse stalks. **3** Halve and stone the avocados, then peel and slice them widthways. Halve the papayas, then remove the seeds and peel and slice the flesh lengthways. **4** Arrange the watercress, avocados and papayas on individual serving plates. Pour the dressing over and serve immediately. For a variation, you can use mangoes instead of the papayas and baby spinach leaves in place of the watercress.

NUTRIENTS PER SERVING KCAL 367 • CARBOHYDRATE 6g (of which 1g sugars) • PROTEIN 3g • FAT 36g (of which saturated fat 6g) • FIBRE 4g • SODIUM 28mg • SALT trace • VEGETABLE PORTION 2

CUCUMBER, RADISH AND MELON SALAD

A wonderful combination of fruit, vegetables and crunchy almonds mixed with a honey and walnut oil dressing, this salad adds a touch of glamour and colour to any meal.

500g piece of watermelon or honeydew melon
100g cucumber
Salt
Olive oil for frying
25g flaked almonds
100g fresh bean sprouts
150g radishes
4 spring onions
A small bunch of watercress

FOR THE DRESSING
1½ teaspoons clear honey
3 tablespoons walnut oil
1 tablespoon cider vinegar
Black pepper

TOTAL TIME 20 minutes
SERVES 4

1 Deseed and dice the melon, then rinse, dry and dice the cucumber. Put both into a colander, add a little salt and toss them together. Place a saucer on top and leave to drain. **2** Heat a little oil in a frying pan and fry the almonds until golden, then drain on kitchen paper. **3** Rinse the bean sprouts and drain them well, then rinse, dry and trim the radishes and spring onions. Quarter the radishes, slice the onions and mix all three together in a salad bowl. **4** Whisk the dressing ingredients together and pour over the salad. **5** Trim the watercress, rinse and dry it and arrange it in a shallow serving dish. Add the melon and cucumber to the salad bowl, toss the salad gently, then spoon it onto the watercress. Scatter the almonds over the top to serve.

NUTRIENTS PER SERVING KCAL 231 • CARBOHYDRATE 15g (of which 14g sugars) • PROTEIN 4g • FAT 18g (of which saturated fat 2g) • FIBRE 2.5g • SODIUM 21mg • SALT trace • VEGETABLE PORTION 2

WATERCRESS, KIWI, MUSHROOM AND TOMATO SALAD

Serve this flavour-packed salad as a vibrant first course or as an accompaniment to a main dish.

125g watercress sprigs
2 kiwi fruit, peeled and thinly sliced
125g button or chestnut mushrooms, thinly
** sliced**
250g tomatoes, sliced

FOR THE DRESSING
1 teaspoon red wine vinegar
Salt and black pepper
4 teaspoons olive oil

PREPARATION TIME 20 minutes
SERVES 4

1 Arrange a bed of watercress in a bowl, then scatter the kiwi fruit, mushrooms and tomatoes on top. **2** To make the dressing, pour the vinegar into a small bowl, season to taste and whisk thoroughly to dissolve the salt. Add the oil and whisk again. **3** Just before serving, pour the dressing over the salad, taking care not to disturb the arrangement.

NUTRIENTS PER SERVING KCAL 64 • CARBOHYDRATE 5g (of which 5g sugars) • PROTEIN 2g
• FAT 4g (of which saturated fat 1g) • FIBRE 2g • SODIUM 24mg • SALT trace
• VEGETABLE PORTION 2

QUINOA SALAD WITH DRIED FRUIT

High in protein and low in fat, quinoa absorbs flavours well and makes a substantial salad.

180g quinoa grains
Salt and black pepper
2 tablespoons pine nuts
1 stick celery, finely diced
50g red onion, finely diced
½ yellow pepper, deseeded and finely diced
12 dried cranberries, snipped into pieces
50g currants

FOR THE DRESSING
½–1 teaspoon ground coriander

½–1 teaspoon ground cumin
1 tablespoon lemon juice
½ teaspoon paprika
1 tablespoon chopped fresh parsley

TO GARNISH fresh flat-leaved parsley

PREPARATION TIME 15 minutes
COOKING TIME 20 minutes
SERVES 4

1 Put a kettle on to boil. Put the quinoa into a large sieve and rinse it thoroughly several times in cold running water to remove its bitter flavour. **2** Put the quinoa in a saucepan with 500ml of boiling water and a pinch of salt and return to the boil. Cover, reduce the heat and simmer for 15 minutes, or until the grains are tender but not mushy. Strain over a large bowl to catch the cooking liquid, then set both aside. **3** Toast the pine nuts in a dry frying pan for 1–2 minutes until they are golden brown. Transfer the quinoa to a large bowl and stir in the celery, onion, pepper, cranberries, currants, and pine nuts. **4** To make the dressing, mix together the coriander, cumin, lemon juice, paprika and parsley. Add up to 4 tablespoons of the quinoa cooking liquid until you have the desired sharpness. Season to taste, then stir it into the salad. Serve, garnished with parsley.

NUTRIENTS PER SERVING KCAL 241 • **CARBOHYDRATE 37g (of which 14g sugars)** • **PROTEIN 8g**
• **FAT 8g (of which saturated fat 1g)** • **FIBRE 1g** • **SODIUM 35mg** • **SALT trace**
• **VEGETABLE PORTION 0**

FRUITY BRUSSELS SPROUTS

Winter vegetables, served raw, make a wonderfully fresh, crunchy and nutritious salad.

225g Brussels sprouts
1 dessert apple
125g carrot, grated
3 celery sticks, chopped
2 tablespoons chopped fresh coriander
125g natural dates, stoned and chopped

FOR THE DRESSING
1 tablespoon half-fat crème fraîche

2 tablespoons reduced-calorie mayonnaise
2 teaspoons olive oil
Grated zest and juice of 1 orange
2 teaspoons white wine vinegar
Salt and black pepper

PREPARATION TIME 25 minutes
SERVES 4

1 To make the dressing, whisk together the crème fraîche, mayonnaise, oil, orange zest and juice and vinegar, then season to taste and set aside. **2** Trim off and discard the bases and outer leaves of the sprouts, then shred them finely and put them into a large bowl. Cut the apple into quarters without peeling it, remove the core then chop into small chunks and add to the bowl with the carrot and celery. **3** Stir in enough dressing to coat the salad, saving any left over to serve on the side. Scatter the coriander and dates over the salad and serve.

NUTRIENTS PER SERVING KCAL 172 • CARBOHYDRATE 30g (of which 29g sugars) • PROTEIN 4g
• FAT 5g (of which saturated fat 1g) • FIBRE 5g • SODIUM 101mg • SALT 0.25g
• VEGETABLE PORTION 2

For the best results, choose firm, bright green Brussels sprouts with tightly packed leaves and no patches of yellow.

CARROT AND GINGER SALAD

A simple salad with a surprising citrus dressing, sharpened with ginger and sweetened with honey, this makes a colourful – and healthy – contribution to any meal.

140g sultanas
400g young carrots
Salt
½ teaspoon honey or sugar
50g chopped peanuts, pecans or walnuts

FOR THE DRESSING
5cm piece fresh root ginger

1 lemon
1 orange
225ml soured cream or 225g natural
  yoghurt

TOTAL TIME 30 minutes
SERVES 4

1 Put a little water into a kettle and put it on to boil. Put the sultanas into a small bowl, then cover them with the boiling water and set them aside. **2** To make the citrus dressing, peel and finely grate the ginger into a small mixing bowl. **3** Wash any wax off the lemon and orange, then finely grate half the rind from each into the bowl. Squeeze the juice from half of each of them and add it to the ginger in the mixing bowl. Stir in the soured cream or yoghurt and set the dressing aside. **4** Peel the carrots and grate them into a serving bowl, then drain the sultanas and add them. **5** Stir the dressing into the carrot and sultana mixture, then season with salt and add honey or sugar to taste. Finally, stir in the chopped nuts and serve.

**NUTRIENTS PER SERVING KCAL 315 • CARBOHYDRATE 35g (of which 33g sugars) • PROTEIN 7g
• FAT 18g (of which saturated fat 8g) • FIBRE 4.5g • SODIUM 57mg • SALT 0.14g
• VEGETABLE PORTION 2**

SPINACH AND BABY CORN SALAD

Succulent morsels of rich avocado are strewn throughout this pretty combination of dark, tender spinach and rocket leaves tossed with tiny cobs of crunchy sweetcorn.

100g baby sweetcorn
Salt
85g rocket leaves
225g baby spinach leaves

FOR THE DRESSING
1 avocado, about 115g
1 clove garlic

3 tablespoons extra virgin olive oil
1 tablespoon white wine vinegar
1 teaspoon sugar
1 teaspoon Tabasco sauce

TOTAL TIME 15 minutes
SERVES 4

1 Bring a small saucepan of water to the boil. Cut the baby sweetcorn across in half and add them to the boiling water with some salt. Simmer for 1 minute then drain. **2** Rinse the rocket and spinach leaves and leave them to drain. **3** Meanwhile, make the dressing. Cut the avocado in half, remove the stone and use a spoon to scoop the flesh into a large salad bowl. **4** Peel the garlic and crush it into the bowl, then add the oil, vinegar, sugar and Tabasco sauce. Season to taste with salt, then stir the dressing together: some of the avocado will merge into the oil, but the diners should find some small chunks in the salad. **5** Add the well-drained sweetcorn, rocket and spinach leaves to the dressing, toss well and serve.

NUTRIENTS PER SERVING KCAL 174 • CARBOHYDRATE 8g (of which 3g sugars) • PROTEIN 3g • FAT 15g (of which saturated fat 3g) • FIBRE 3g • SODIUM 96mg • SALT 0.2g • VEGETABLE PORTION 2

BEETROOT WITH HORSERADISH CREAM DRESSING

With a vibrant, deep ruby-red colour and a fresh flavour and texture, raw beetroot tastes completely different from beetroot pickled in malt vinegar. It makes a spectacular salad.

675g raw beetroot, peeled
1 small red onion, finely chopped
1 tablespoon sunflower oil
2 tablespoons orange juice
2 teaspoon red wine vinegar
150g small salad leaves, such as beetroot
  tops, baby chard, lamb's lettuce, red
  mustard, mizuna, baby spinach or sorrel

HORSERADISH DRESSING
3 tablespoons soured cream

3 tablespoons plain low-fat yoghurt
1 teaspoon grated fresh horseradish or
  2 teaspoons horseradish sauce
2 tablespoons chopped fresh dill
salt and pepper

PREPARATION TIME 20 minutes, plus
  30 minutes marinating
SERVES 4

1 Grate the beetroot into a mixing bowl, keeping all the juices (this can also be done in a food processor with a coarse grating disc). Add the onion and stir to mix with the beetroot.
2 Whisk together the oil, orange juice and vinegar in a small bowl. Season with salt and pepper to taste. Pour it over the beetroot and onion and toss well. Cover and leave to marinate at room temperature for 30 minutes. (The salad can be prepared up to this stage and kept for up to 24 hours in the fridge.) **3** Put the salad leaves into a serving bowl. Add the marinated beetroot and onion and toss together. **4** For the dressing, stir the soured cream, yoghurt, horseradish and dill together. Spoon the dressing on the salad and serve immediately.

NUTRIENTS PER SERVING KCAL 181 • CARBOHYDRATE 18g (of which 16g sugars)
• PROTEIN 5g • FAT 10g (of which saturated fat 3g) • FIBRE 4g • SODIUM 148mg
• SALT 0.37g • VEGETABLE PORTION 2

Eating onions, whether cooked or raw, may help to reduce blood cholesterol by increasing levels of the lipoproteins that help carry cholesterol away from body tissues.

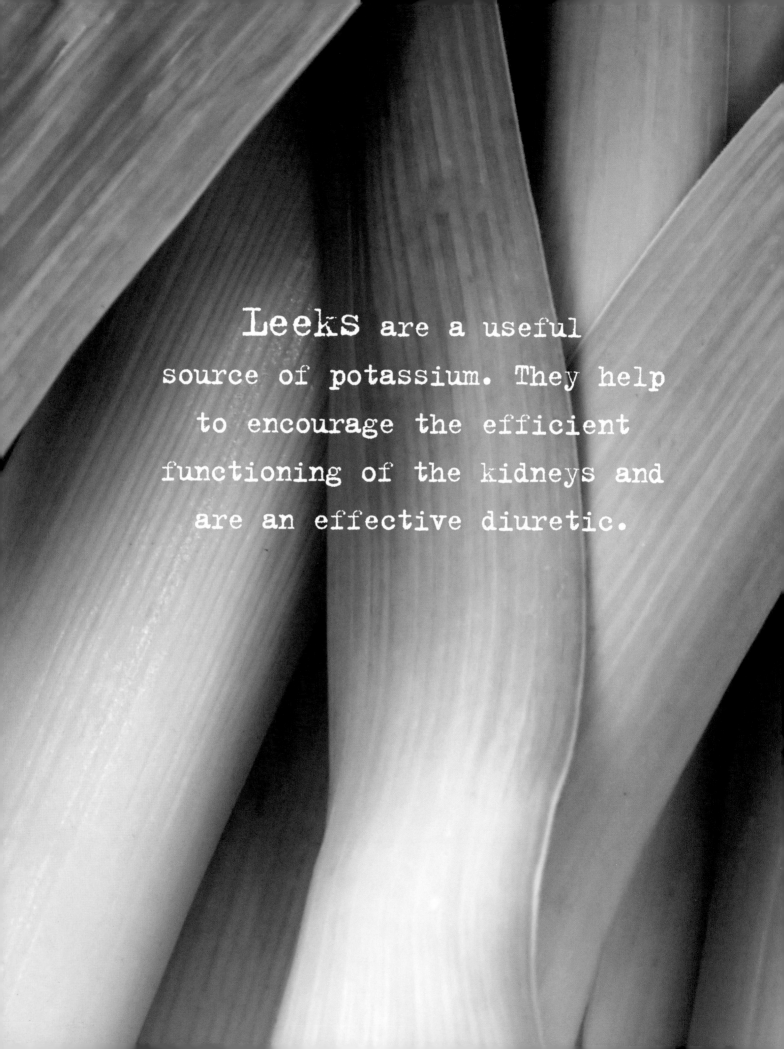

Leeks are a useful
source of potassium. They help
to encourage the efficient
functioning of the kidneys and
are an effective diuretic.

MARINATED LEEKS

Enjoy this simple salad with its herb and mustard dressing as a light first course or tasty side dish.

8 slim young leeks
Salt and black pepper

FOR THE MARINADE
2 tablespoons extra virgin olive oil
2 teaspoons white wine vinegar
1 tablespoon wholegrain mustard
2 tablespoons finely chopped fresh chives
2 tablespoons finely chopped fresh parsley
1 teaspoon finely chopped fresh tarragon

TO GARNISH 4 sprigs of fresh tarragon

TO SERVE wholemeal bread slices, optional

**PREPARATION TIME 20 minutes, plus
  30 minutes marinating**
COOKING TIME 10 minutes
SERVES 4

1 Bring a wide pan of salted water to the boil. Cut the leeks lengthways or, for a dinner party presentation, cut a cross from the top of each leek through the leaves to halfway down the white part of the stem. Rinse the cut leeks in lots of cold water to remove any grit. **2** Drop half the leeks into the boiling water and boil them for 4–5 minutes until they are tender. Remove with a slotted spoon and cool them under cold water. Drain and pat them dry then arrange them in a shallow dish. Repeat with the remaining leeks. **3** Meanwhile, to make the marinade, whisk together the oil, vinegar, mustard and herbs and season to taste. Spoon the mixture over the leeks then use your hands to turn them so that they are well coated. Cover and leave to marinate at room temperature for 30 minutes, turning occasionally. **4** If serving as a starter, divide the leeks among four plates, fan out the leaves if cut crossways, and garnish with tarragon.

NUTRIENTS PER SERVING KCAL 81 • CARBOHYDRATE 3g (of which 3g sugars) • PROTEIN 2g • FAT 6g (of which saturated fat 1g) • FIBRE 4g • SODIUM 4mg • SALT trace • VEGETABLE PORTION 2

CARROT AND RADISH RICE SALAD WITH TOFU DRESSING

Brown rice tossed with crisp vegetables and fresh and dried fruit makes an unusual side salad. The almost fat-free dressing is based on tofu, which gives it a grainy texture similar to the Greek dip, hummus. For a smoother mayonnaise-like texture, use silken tofu.

200g long-grain brown rice
125g radishes, sliced
1 large carrot, cut into matchsticks
2 spring onions, chopped
1 Asian pear, peeled, cored and diced
55g raisins
4 tablespoons coarsely chopped fresh coriander

TOFU DRESSING
125g tofu, diced

2 teaspoons Dijon mustard
1 tablespoon white wine vinegar
1 garlic clove, crushed
3 tablespoons orange juice
salt and pepper

PREPARATION AND COOKING TIME 50 minutes,
  plus cooling
SERVES 4

1 Put the rice in a saucepan, add 600ml water and bring to the boil. Cover and simmer very gently for 30–40 minutes or until the rice is tender and has absorbed all the water. Remove from the heat and leave to cool. **2** While the rice is cooling, make the dressing. Put the tofu into a blender or food processor, add the mustard, vinegar, garlic and orange juice, and blend until smooth. Season with salt and pepper to taste. **3** Pour the tofu dressing into a large bowl. Add the radishes, carrot, spring onions, Asian pear, raisins and chopped coriander, and stir until well combined, then stir in the rice. Serve at room temperature or lightly chilled.

NUTRIENTS PER SERVING KCAL 277 • CARBOHYDRATE 58g (of which 17g sugars) • PROTEIN 7g
• FAT 3g (of which saturated fat 0.5g) • FIBRE 3g • SODIUM 22mg • SALT trace
• VEGETABLE PORTION 1

RATATOUILLE CHINESE-STYLE

This vegetable salad is given a piquant flavour with Oriental black bean and hoisin sauces.

125g courgettes
125g aubergine
125g small chestnut, oyster or shiitake
mushrooms
125g tomatoes, peeled, deseeded and cut into
small dice
125g canned water chestnuts, drained and
sliced

FOR THE DRESSING
1 tablespoon black bean sauce
1 tablespoon hoisin sauce
2 tablespoons dry sherry
A few drops of Tabasco sauce
1 teaspoon red or white wine vinegar

PREPARATION TIME 25 minutes, plus 20
minutes marinating
COOKING TIME 8 minutes
SERVES 2 as a main course, 4 as a side dish

1 Put a kettle on to boil. To make the dressing, put all the ingredients into a bowl, mix together and set aside. **2** Heat the grill to high. Cut the courgettes in half lengthways and then into 2cm chunks. Blanch them in boiling water for 2 minutes, then drain and refresh them under running cold water. Dry them on kitchen paper. **3** Cut the aubergine into 1cm slices. Cook the slices on a baking tray under the grill for 3 minutes on each side, or until they are tender. Leave them to cool, then cut them into quarters. **4** Grill the mushrooms for 5 minutes, turning occasionally, then set them aside to cool. **5** Put the vegetables into a serving dish and add the tomatoes and water chestnuts. Pour the dressing over them, mix well and set aside to marinate for 20 minutes for the flavours to blend (do not refrigerate). **6** As a salad, serve the ratatouille at room temperature. As a side dish, tip the dressed salad into a hot, nonstick wok or frying pan and stir-fry over a high heat for 5–8 minutes, until steaming hot. Serve as a part of a vegetarian meal.

NUTRIENTS PER SERVING KCAL 91 • CARBOHYDRATE 12g (of which 8g sugars) • PROTEIN 5g
• FAT 1g (of which saturated fat 1g) • FIBRE 4g • SODIUM 520mg • SALT 1.3g
• VEGETABLE PORTION 2

ROASTED POTATO SALAD WITH CUMIN AND YOGHURT DRESSING

This hot potato salad is served with a lightly spiced, cool dressing – for a refreshing difference.

1 tablespoon olive oil
Salt and black pepper
5 small baking potatoes, scrubbed
125g mixed salad leaves

FOR THE DRESSING
½ teaspoon ground cumin

Juice of ½ lemon
100g lite Greek yoghurt

PREPARATION TIME 15 minutes
COOKING TIME 50–55 minutes
SERVES 4

1 Heat the oven to 200°C (400°F, gas mark 6). In a bowl, stir together the oil and ½ teaspoon salt, then use your hands to turn and coat the potatoes in the mixture. Place the potatoes on a baking tray and roast for 50–55 minutes until soft when squeezed and crisp on the outside. **2** To make the dressing, place the cumin in a small ovenproof dish, such as a ramekin, and toast it in the hot oven for no more than 2 minutes while the potatoes are roasting. Do not let it burn. Remove it from the oven and leave it to cool. **3** In a small bowl, stir together the cooled cumin, lemon juice and yoghurt and add salt and pepper to taste. Cover and chill, or set aside in a cool room.
4 Arrange the salad leaves on four serving plates. When the potatoes are done, remove them from the oven and, using an oven mitt for protection, quarter them lengthways into wedges.
5 Put five potato wedges on each plate. Drizzle the warm potatoes with the dressing and serve.

NUTRIENTS PER SERVING KCAL 189 • **CARBOHYDRATE 32g (of which 3g sugars)** • **PROTEIN 5g**
• **FAT 5g (of which saturated fat 2g)** • **FIBRE 3.5g** • **SODIUM 21mg** • **SALT trace**
• **VEGETABLE PORTION 0**

GRILLED VEGETABLE SALAD

Succulent vegetable juices and sherry vinegar moisten this salad so that you do not need an oily dressing. It is best made the day before, to allow the flavours to develop fully.

350g aubergines
700g courgettes
Salt and black pepper
1 large red pepper, cut into quarters
2 tablespoons olive oil

FOR THE DRESSING
A pinch of cayenne pepper

2 cloves garlic, crushed
1 tablespoon sherry vinegar

TO GARNISH chopped fresh parsley

PREPARATION TIME 15 minutes, plus at least
  3 hours standing
COOKING TIME 20–35 minutes
SERVES 4

1 Line two baking trays with kitchen paper. Cut the aubergine and courgettes lengthways into 2cm thick slices, put them on the trays in a single layer and sprinkle with salt. Set aside for 15 minutes. **2** Meanwhile, make the dressing. Mix the cayenne, garlic, and vinegar together, season to taste and set aside. **3** Heat a ridged, cast-iron grill pan over a medium-high heat or set the grill to medium-high. Brush the skin side of the pepper with oil and cook the pieces, skin side down on the grill pan or skin side up under the grill, for 5 minutes, or until the pepper has softened and the skin has blackened a little. **4** Place the pepper in a large bowl, sprinkle over one-third of the dressing and stir. **5** Rinse the aubergine and courgette slices and pat them dry, then brush them lightly with oil. Grill for 3–4 minutes on each side for the aubergines and 2–3 minutes on each side for the courgettes. (You will need to cook them in batches if you are using a ridged grill pan.) **6** Cut the grilled aubergine and courgette slices in half crossways and add them to the pepper. Pour on the remaining dressing and mix well. **7** Cover and refrigerate for at least 3 hours, or overnight. Serve at room temperature.

NUTRIENTS PER SERVING KCAL 106 • CARBOHYDRATE 8g (of which 7g sugars) • PROTEIN 4g • FAT 7g (of which saturated fat 1g) • FIBRE 4g • SODIUM 35mg • SALT trace • VEGETABLE PORTION 3

CHINESE-STYLE HOT NOODLE SALAD WITH VEGETABLES

Fragrant ginger and lemongrass flavour this hearty vegetable and noodle salad.

100g thin egg noodles
2 teaspoons sunflower oil
1 fresh red chilli, deseeded and finely chopped
2–3 cloves garlic, chopped
2 tablespoons finely grated ginger
1 tablespoon lemongrass, very finely chopped
200g carrots, cut into matchsticks
1 red pepper, diced
1 yellow pepper, diced
150g baby sweetcorn, cut in half lengthways
100g sugarsnap peas
250g Chinese leaves, finely shredded
6 spring onions, finely sliced
4 tablespoons soy sauce
1 teaspoon sesame oil
3 tablespoons fresh coriander leaves
25g salted peanuts, finely chopped

PREPARATION TIME 30 minutes
COOKING TIME 10 minutes
SERVES 4

1 Put a kettle on to boil. Cook the noodles in boiling water according to the instructions on the packet, then drain them well. **2** Heat the sunflower oil in a hot wok or large frying pan and stir-fry the chilli, garlic, ginger, lemongrass, carrots, peppers, sweetcorn and sugarsnap peas for 4–5 minutes. **3** Add the Chinese leaves, spring onions, drained noodles, soy sauce and sesame oil. Toss everything together over a medium heat for a further minute until they are thoroughly combined and hot. **4** Finally, add the coriander and peanuts, toss together once more and serve.

NUTRIENTS PER SERVING KCAL 236 • **CARBOHYDRATE 36g (of which 14g sugars)** • **PROTEIN 9g** • **FAT 9g (of which saturated fat 2g)** • **FIBRE 5g** • **SODIUM 1180mg** • **SALT 3g** • **VEGETABLE PORTION 2**

WILD RICE AND FENNEL SALAD

Grapes, orange and a handful of raisins add sweetness to a salad brimming with the earthy flavours of wild rice, chopped hazelnuts and a nut oil, herb and white wine vinegar dressing.

175g American easy-cook wild rice and long grain mixture
Salt
250g cucumber
250g Florence fennel
6 spring onions
125g seedless ruby grapes
50g skinned hazelnuts
25g raisins
1 orange

FOR THE DRESSING
3 sprigs of chervil
2 sprigs each of tarragon and parsley
6 tablespoons hazelnut or walnut oil
1 tablespoon white wine vinegar
Salt and black pepper

TO GARNISH 4–6 sprigs tarragon

TIME 30 minutes
SERVES 4–6

1 Bring 425ml of water to the boil, add the rice and a little salt, cover and simmer for about 18–20 minutes, or until the rice is cooked and all the water absorbed. **2** Meanwhile, rinse and dry the cucumber, fennel, spring onions and grapes. Finely dice the cucumber; trim and thinly slice the fennel and spring onions and halve the grapes. Put them all into a salad bowl. Chop the hazelnuts and add them, with the raisins. **3** Wash any wax from the orange and grate the rind into the salad. **4** To make the herb dressing, squeeze 3 tablespoons of juice from the orange and pour it into a small bowl. Rinse, dry and finely chop the herbs and add them to the juice with the oil and vinegar. Whisk together then season to taste. **5** Drain the cooked rice and rinse it briefly under a cold tap. Drain well, mix it into the salad vegetables and pour the dressing over. Garnish with sprigs of tarragon.

NUTRIENTS PER SERVING KCAL 459 • CARBOHYDRATE 50g (of which 12g sugars) • PROTEIN 7g • FAT 26g (of which saturated fat 2g) • FIBRE 4g • SODIUM 17mg • SALT trace • VEGETABLE PORTION 2

Nuts can supply many of the nutrients that can be missing from a vegetarian diet. **Walnuts** may help to reduce the risk of coronary heart disease.

GRILLED CHICORY, STILTON AND WALNUT SALAD

Grilling adds a lovely smoky flavour to the chicory in a nutritious salad that includes the classic British duo of Stilton and heart-healthy walnuts. Serve warm, for sophisticated comfort food.

**4 small or 2 large chicory heads, halved
lengthways and cores removed**
Vegetable oil for brushing
**1 large Conference or Williams pear, peeled,
cored and sliced**
2 tablespoons walnut oil
Salt and black pepper

100g Stilton cheese, finely crumbled
25g walnut halves, lightly toasted

PREPARATION TIME 5 minutes
COOKING TIME 8–13 minutes
SERVES 4

1 Heat the grill to very hot. Brush the chicory lightly with vegetable oil and place on the grill rack, cut side up. Grill them as near to the heat as possible for 2–3 minutes for smaller heads (3–4 minutes for larger heads) until beginning to soften and char. Turn, then brush lightly with oil and continue to cook for 2–3 minutes (or 3–4 minutes) until softened and lightly charred.
2 Turn the chicory over again to cut side up. Lay the pear slices on the chicory, brush lightly with walnut oil, sprinkle with salt and pepper and return to the grill for 4–5 minutes to warm the pears. **3** Transfer to warmed plates, sprinkle with the Stilton and toasted walnuts and drizzle with the remaining walnut oil. Serve at once.

**NUTRIENTS PER SERVING KCAL 235 • CARBOHYDRATE 4g (of which 3g sugars) • PROTEIN 7g
• FAT 21g (of which saturated fat 7g) • FIBRE 1g • SODIUM 199mg • SALT 0.5g
• VEGETABLE PORTION 0**

RUSSIAN BEAN SALAD

Beetroot, soya beans and potatoes are tossed in a piquant sour cream dressing, then served on a salad of rocket, fennel and tomatoes in this delicious and refreshing main course salad. Serve with dark rye bread so you can mop up all the creamy dressing.

150g dried soya beans, soaked overnight
450g small new potatoes, scrubbed and halved
2 large shallots, thinly sliced
250g peeled, cooked beetroot (not pickled), diced
500g tomatoes, sliced
1 bulb of fennel, thinly sliced
55g rocket
salt and pepper

SOURED CREAM DRESSING
150ml soured cream
150g plain low-fat yoghurt
4 sweet and sour gherkins, finely chopped
2 tablespoon creamed horseradish
1 teaspoon caster sugar

PREPARATION AND COOKING TIME 3¼ hours, plus cooling
SERVES 4

1 Drain the soaked beans and rinse under cold running water. Put in a saucepan and cover with fresh water. Bring to the boil and boil rapidly for 10–15 minutes, then partly cover and simmer for about 2½ hours or until tender. Drain and leave to cool. **2** Put the potatoes into a saucepan of boiling water and simmer for about 15 minutes or until just tender. Drain and leave until cool enough to handle. **3** Meanwhile, for the dressing, mix together the soured cream and yoghurt in a large mixing bowl. Stir in the chopped gherkins, horseradish, sugar, and salt and pepper to taste. **4** Add the soya beans and shallots to the bowl and stir into the dressing. Cut the warm potatoes into cubes and add to the bean mixture, then gently fold in the beetroot. **5** Divide the tomatoes, fennel and rocket among 4 serving plates. Spoon the soya bean salad on top and serve immediately.

NUTRIENTS PER SERVING KCAL 386 • CARBOHYDRATE 41g (of which 20g sugars) • PROTEIN 21g • FAT 16g (of which saturated fat 6g) • FIBRE 11g • SODIUM 206mg • SALT 0.5g • VEGETABLE PORTION 3

WARM FLAGEOLET AND CHARRED VEGETABLE SALAD

Balsamic vinegar enhances the strong flavours of the vegetables in this warm, piquant salad, excellent served as a light lunch – and you can ring the changes with a good wine or cider vinegar.

1 red pepper
1 yellow pepper
1 medium onion
2 medium courgettes
2 tablespoons olive oil
420g canned flageolet beans
420g canned lentils
2 large sprigs of basil
2 medium tomatoes
2 tablespoons crushed sun-dried tomatoes
   in oil
1 tablespoon balsamic vinegar
Salt and black pepper

TO GARNISH 12 large black olives

TOTAL TIME 20 minutes
SERVES 4

1 Rinse, deseed and roughly chop the peppers. Peel and slice the onion. Trim, rinse, dry and thinly slice the courgettes. **2** Heat the oil in a large frying pan and brown the peppers, onion and courgettes over a high heat, stirring occasionally. **3** Meanwhile, drain and rinse the canned beans and lentils. Rinse, dry and tear the basil leaves, and rinse, dry and roughly chop the fresh tomatoes. **4** Add the beans and lentils to the pan, stir gently, then add the basil, the fresh tomatoes, the sun-dried tomatoes and the vinegar. **5** Season the mixture, then let it heat through, stirring well. Stone the olives if necessary. **6** Turn the salad into a warm dish, garnish with the olives and serve immediately.

NUTRIENTS PER SERVING KCAL 390 • CARBOHYDRATE 52g (of which 9g sugars) • PROTEIN 21g • FAT 11g (of which saturated fat 1g) • FIBRE 12g • SODIUM 402mg • SALT 1g • VEGETABLE PORTION 2

GRILLED GOAT'S CHEESE SALAD

Crisp toasted French bread is spread with a rich red onion marmalade flavoured with balsamic vinegar and rosemary, topped with creamy goat's cheese and finished under the grill. Served with a beetroot, pepper and lamb's lettuce salad, it makes an impressive starter or snack lunch.

1 tablespoon extra virgin olive oil
4 small red onions, about 300g in total, thinly sliced
2 garlic cloves, finely chopped
1 teaspoon sugar
2 teaspoons balsamic vinegar
4 slices French bread, about 115g in total
few sprigs of fresh rosemary
200g goat's cheese, cut into 4 slices
85g lamb's lettuce

115g cooked beetroot, peeled and cut into thin strips
1 small red pepper, seeded and cut into thin strips
salt and pepper
Balsamic dressing
2 tablespoons extra virgin olive oil
2 teaspoons balsamic vinegar

PREPARATION TIME 25 minutes
SERVES 4

1 Preheat the grill. Heat the oil in a frying pan, add the onions and cook for 5 minutes, stirring occasionally, until softened. Add the garlic and sugar, and cook for a further 5–8 minutes, stirring frequently, until the onions are very soft, browned and caramelised. Stir in the balsamic vinegar. **2** Lightly toast the French bread on both sides under the grill. Divide the onion marmalade among the slices. Top each with a few rosemary leaves and then a slice of goat's cheese. Add a sprinkling of pepper. **3** Cook the cheesy toasts under the hot grill for 3–4 minutes or until the cheese is bubbling. **4** Meanwhile, to make the dressing, whisk the oil, vinegar and salt and pepper to taste in a mixing bowl. Add the lamb's lettuce, beetroot and red pepper and toss. Divide among four plates. Top with the goat's cheese toasts, garnish with rosemary and serve.

NUTRIENTS PER SERVING KCAL 372 • CARBOHYDRATE 30g (of which 12.5g sugars) • PROTEIN 15g • FAT 22g (of which saturated fat 10g) • FIBRE 3g • SODIUM 513mg • SALT 1.3g • VEGETABLE PORTION 2

GREEK SALAD

A pretty variation on the classic Mediterranean salad mixes sweet cherry tomatoes with salty feta cheese and olives to make a colourful, healthy and delicious addition to any meal.

20 cherry tomatoes
1 cucumber
375g Greek feta cheese
4 tablespoons extra virgin olive oil
½ lemon

12 good black olives
Black pepper

TOTAL TIME 15 minutes
SERVES 4–6

1 Rinse and dry the cherry tomatoes, then cut them in half and place them in a serving bowl. Rinse, dry and halve the cucumber, then cut each half into 1cm slices and add them to the tomatoes. **2** Drain the cheese and crumble it into the bowl. Sprinkle in the oil and 1 tablespoon of juice from the half lemon. Add the black olives and pepper to taste (the cheese is salty already). Toss well and serve.

NUTRIENTS PER SERVING KCAL 365 • **CARBOHYDRATE 5g (of which 5g sugars)** • **PROTEIN 16g** • **FAT 31g (of which saturated fat 15g)** • **FIBRE 1.5g** • **SODIUM 1448mg** • **SALT 3.6g** • **VEGETABLE PORTION 1**

Both black and green olives are low in calories and high in vitamin E. Olive oil may also help to lower cholesterol levels.

BEAN SPROUT, FETA AND HAZELNUT SALAD

A nutritious mix of crunchy salad vegetables, salty white cheese, fresh citrus fruit and roasted hazelnuts with a tangy orange and nut oil dressing makes a great salad for the winter months.

5cm piece of cucumber
2 sticks celery
350g fresh bean sprouts, or a mixture of mung
  and alfalfa sprouts
100g hazelnut kernels, ready-skinned
1 orange
150g Greek feta cheese

TO GARNISH 1 punnet salad cress

FOR THE DRESSING
1 orange
2 tablespoons hazelnut, or walnut, oil
Salt and black pepper
1 teaspoon wholegrain mustard

TOTAL TIME 20 minutes
SERVES 4

1 Preheat the oven to 200°C (400°F, gas mark 6) and bring a saucepan of water to the boil.
2 Rinse and dry the cucumber and celery, chop them into small pieces and place in a salad bowl.
3 Place the bean or mung sprouts in the boiling water for 1 minute to blanch, then drain and rinse. Alfalfa sprouts do not need blanching. **4** Press the hazelnuts in half with a rolling pin. Toast on a tray in the oven for 3–4 minutes until golden. **5** Cut the peel and pith from the orange then, holding it over the celery to catch any juice, cut the segments from the connecting tissue and let them fall into the bowl. **6** To make the dressing, squeeze the juice from the orange into a small bowl or jug and whisk in the nut oil, seasoning and mustard. **7** Drain the cheese and crumble it into the salad bowl, then add the bean sprouts and hazelnuts. Rinse and dry the cress. Pour the dressing onto the salad, toss gently and garnish with cress.

NUTRIENTS PER SERVING KCAL 352 • CARBOHYDRATE 9g (of which 7g sugars) • PROTEIN 13g • FAT 30g (of which saturated fat 7g) • FIBRE 2.5g • SODIUM 553mg • SALT 1.4g • VEGETABLE PORTION 0

STILTON, PEAR AND WATERCRESS SALAD

The ingredients of this fresh and colourful salad, with contrasting colours, textures and flavours, are perfectly complemented by the subtle walnut oil dressing and lightly toasted walnut pieces. Serve for a tempting lunch, accompanied by crusty wholegrain rolls or bread.

55g walnut pieces
1 red onion, thinly sliced
3 large, ripe dessert pears, preferably
  red-skinned
115g watercress
115g Stilton cheese, crumbled
pepper

WALNUT AND POPPY SEED DRESSING
½ teaspoon Dijon mustard
2 teaspoons red wine vinegar
1 tablespoon sunflower oil
1 tablespoon walnut oil
2 teaspoons poppy seeds

PREPARATION TIME 15 minutes
SERVES 4

1 First make the dressing. Stir the mustard and vinegar together in a salad bowl with pepper to taste, then gradually whisk in the sunflower and walnuts oils. Stir in the poppy seeds. Set aside while preparing the salad. **2** Lightly toast the walnut pieces in a small frying pan, stirring them frequently. Leave to cool. **3** Add the red onion to the salad bowl and mix with the dressing. Quarter, core and slice the pears, leaving the skins on. Add to the bowl and toss gently to coat with the dressing. **4** Add the watercress and most of the cheese and walnuts to the pears. Toss together gently, then scatter the remaining cheese and nuts over the top, and serve immediately.

NUTRIENTS PER SERVING KCAL 348 • CARBOHYDRATE 22g (of which 21g sugars) • PROTEIN 10g • FAT 26g (of which saturated fat 7g) • FIBRE 6g • SODIUM 500mg • SALT 1.2g • VEGETABLE PORTION 2

SUGARSNAP SALAD WITH BLACK GRAPES AND FETA CHEESE

Sugarsnap peas, with their full flavour and crisp texture, work well with baby spinach leaves and a little peppery rocket to provide the salad base for tangy feta cheese and sweet black grapes. Serve this quickly prepared lunch dish with thick slices of warm country-style or pitta bread.

grated zest and juice of d lemon
½ teaspoon caster sugar
½ teaspoon Dijon mustard
1 tablespoon extra virgin olive oil
300g sugarsnap peas
200g seedless black grapes, halved
200g feta cheese, cut into thin slices

45g rocket, shredded
170g baby spinach leaves
salt and pepper

PREPARATION TIME about 20 minutes
SERVES 4

1 Place the lemon zest and juice in a large salad bowl. Add the sugar and mustard with salt and pepper to taste. Whisk the ingredients together until the sugar and salt have dissolved in the lemon juice. Whisk in the olive oil. **2** Cut the sugarsnap peas across in half. Bring a large pan of water to the boil, add the sugarsnap peas and bring back to the boil. Immediately drain the sugarsnaps and refresh under cold running water. Add them to the salad bowl, and turn and fold to coat them with the dressing. **3** Add the grapes, feta cheese, rocket and spinach to the bowl, and mix the salad gently but well, so that all the ingredients are coated with dressing. Serve at once.

NUTRIENTS PER SERVING KCAL 221 • CARBOHYDRATE 14g (of which 13g sugars) • PROTEIN 12g • FAT 14g (of which saturated fat 7g) • FIBRE 3g • SODIUM 785mg • SALT 1.9g • VEGETABLE PORTION 2

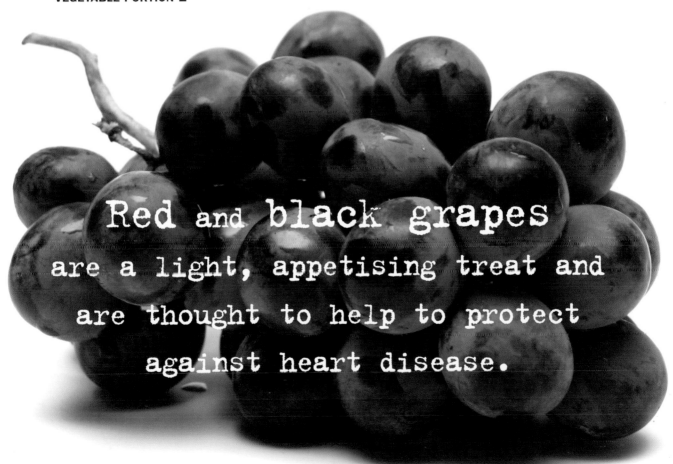

Red and black grapes are a light, appetising treat and are thought to help to protect against heart disease.

MELTED BRIE WITH VEGETABLES

In this unusual salad, a creamy dressing, made from melted brie cheese delicately flavoured with tarragon, is spooned over spicy roasted potato wedges, baby plum tomatoes, green beans and red onion. It seems a very indulgent dish, but makes a healthy main meal.

100g thin green beans, halved
900g baking potatoes, scrubbed and cut into big wedges
1½ tablespoons extra virgin olive oil
1 teaspoon paprika
1 teaspoon salt flakes
few coarsely crushed black peppercorns
2 tablespoons sesame seeds
1 small iceberg lettuce, torn into bite-sized pieces
1 red onion, thinly sliced
½ cucumber, chopped

225g baby plum or cherry tomatoes, halved
juice of 1 lemon
salt and pepper

BRIE DRESSING
250g brie, rind removed and diced
4 tablespons semi-skimmed milk
1 tablespoon finely chopped fresh tarragon

PREPARATION AND COOKING TIME about 1 hour
SERVES 4

1 Preheat the oven to 200°C (400°F, gas mark 6) and put in a roasting tin to heat. Drop the beans into a large saucepan of boiling water and blanch for 2 minutes. Using a draining spoon, scoop the beans out of the pan into a colander, and refresh under cold running water. Add the potatoes to the saucepan of boiling water and cook for 3 minutes, then drain. **2** Put the potato wedges in a bowl. Add the oil, paprika, salt flakes and crushed peppercorns, and toss to coat the potatoes. Tip them into the hot roasting tin. Roast for about 15 minutes. Sprinkle with the sesame seeds and roast for a further 30 minutes, turning once or twice, until crisp and browned. **3** When the potatoes are ready, remove from the oven and keep hot. Put the beans, lettuce, onion, cucumber and tomatoes in a mixing bowl. Add the lemon juice and salt and pepper to taste, and toss well.
4 To make the dressing, put the brie and milk into a saucepan and heat gently, stirring, until melted and well blended. Stir in the tarragon and a little pepper, and cook for a few seconds.
5 Spoon the bean and tomato salad into four bowls. Top with the roasted potatoes and spoon the warm brie dressing over them. Serve at once.

NUTRIENTS PER SERVING KCAL 491 • CARBOHYDRATE 48g (of which 8g sugars) • PROTEIN 21g • FAT 26g (of which saturated fat 9g) • FIBRE 6g • SODIUM 673mg • SALT 1.6g • VEGETABLE PORTION 1

the side

ON THE SIDE

Not only is **beetroot** rich in potassium and a good source of folate, but boiled or roasted, it retains all its valuable minerals and a wealth of vitamins, including vitamin C.

BEETROOT IN BÉCHAMEL

Colourful, tender slices of beetroot are topped with crumbly chestnuts and tangy spring onions, all under a satisfying white sauce. Serve as a whole, or in individual dishes.

4 beetroot, about 85g each
115g frozen chestnuts
½ tablespoon sunflower oil
6 spring onions, trimmed and cut into
  4cm lengths
1 small clove garlic, crushed
15g butter

15g plain flour
175ml semi-skimmed milk
Salt and black pepper

PREPARATION TIME 35–40 minutes
COOKING TIME about 1 hour
SERVES 4

1 Put the beetroot into a large saucepan, cover with water and bring to the boil. Cover and simmer for about 45 minutes until tender. Drain and set aside to cool. **2** Put the chestnuts in a small pan, add water and simmer for 5-6 minutes until tender. **3** Heat the oil in a small frying pan and fry the spring onion and garlic for 2-3 minutes until softened. Remove from the heat and stir in the chestnuts, pressing them with the back of a spoon or spatula so that they crumble slightly. **4** Trim the top and bottom of the beetroot and peel. Slice thinly and arrange in the bottom of a shallow, ovenproof dish. Sprinkle over the spring onion and chestnut mixture. **5** Melt the butter in a small saucepan, stir in the flour and then gradually add the milk to make a fairly thin sauce. Add salt and pepper to taste. **6** Pour the sauce over the beetroot and chestnuts. Heat the grill and set the dish under the grill for about 5 minutes until the top is golden and bubbly. Serve at once, as it is, or as a side dish with a main meal.

NUTRIENTS PER SERVING KCAL 150 • CARBOHYDRATE 22g (of which 10g sugars) • PROTEIN 4g • FAT 6g (of which saturated fat 3g) • FIBRE 3g • SODIUM 103mg • SALT 0.2g • VEGETABLE PORTION 1

AUBERGINES WITH TAHINI DRESSING

Lightly steamed aubergines spiked with spring onions and sun-dried tomatoes are served in a Middle Eastern dressing of sesame-based tahini, making an unusual alternative to cream or butter sauces.

400g aubergines
4 spring onions
25g sun-dried tomatoes in oil

FOR THE DRESSING
1 clove garlic
1 lemon
1 tablespoon tahini paste

3 tablespoons olive oil
Salt and black pepper

TO GARNISH a few sprigs of fresh dill

TOTAL TIME 25 minutes
SERVES 4

1 Fill a steamer with water and bring it to the boil. **2** Trim and rinse the aubergines. Halve them lengthways if they are large, then cut them widthways into slices about 5mm thick. Put them into the steamer, cover and cook for 6–8 minutes, or until they have softened. **3** To make the dressing, peel the garlic and crush it into a small bowl, then squeeze 3 tablespoons of juice from the lemon and add it to the garlic. Add the tahini paste and olive oil, season to taste and mix. **4** Trim, rinse, and thinly slice the spring onions, drain and chop the sun-dried tomatoes and set them aside. **5** Transfer the cooked aubergines to a colander and press them down firmly with a spoon to remove as much of their juice as possible – do not worry if they break up. Then transfer them to a serving bowl and stir in the spring onions and the sun-dried tomatoes. **6** Pour over the tahini dressing and toss well. Rinse, dry and chop enough dill to give 1 tablespoon and scatter it over the aubergines. Leave them to cool for 5 minutes to let the flavour develop before serving, accompanied by some hot crusty bread.

NUTRIENTS PER SERVING KCAL 140 • CARBOHYDRATE 4g (of which 2g sugars) • PROTEIN 2g • FAT 13g (of which saturated fat 3g) • FIBRE 2g • SODIUM 4mg • SALT trace • VEGETABLE PORTION 1

SOY-DRESSED GREEN BEANS

Young, thin beans are tossed in soy sauce with fresh ginger in this stylish side dish. To ring the changes, substitute sliced carrots, runner beans or baby sweetcorn, adjusting the cooking time.

500g green beans
Salt
2 cloves garlic, finely chopped
½ teaspoon finely chopped ginger
2 tablespoons soy sauce

½ teaspoon sugar

PREPARATION TIME 10 minutes
COOKING TIME 5 minutes
SERVES 4

1 Line up the green beans in bunches and cut them in half crossways. **2** Bring a saucepan of water to the boil, then add the beans and a pinch of salt and return to the boil. Reduce the heat and simmer for 3 minutes, or until the beans are tender. **3** Place the garlic, ginger, soy sauce and sugar in a serving bowl and stir them together until the sugar has dissolved. Drain the beans, toss them into the dressing, then serve.

NUTRIENTS PER SERVING KCAL 32 • CARBOHYDRATE 5g (of which 3g sugars) • PROTEIN 2g • FAT 1g (no saturated fat) • FIBRE 3g • SODIUM 534mg • SALT 1.3g • VEGETABLE PORTION 1

Cabbage may help to prevent cancer of the colon and offer relief for painful gastric ulcers. It is also provides vitamins C, E and K.

STIR-FRIED CABBAGE AND SPRING GREENS

White cabbage contrasts with dark spring greens in this easy stir-fry, while crunchy cashew nuts, root ginger and celery add oriental flavour.

350g white cabbage
350g spring greens
2 cloves garlic
2cm piece fresh root ginger
2 sticks celery
4 spring onions

2 tablespoons sesame oil
55g unsalted cashew nuts

TO SERVE light soy sauce

TOTAL TIME 20 minutes
SERVES 4–6

1 Trim, rinse, dry and shred the white cabbage and spring greens. Peel and chop the garlic, peel and grate the ginger, and rinse, dry and slice the celery and spring onions. **2** Heat the sesame oil in a large frying pan and fry the cashew nuts for 30 seconds, until they are just beginning to turn brown. **3** Add the garlic, ginger, celery and spring onions and cook them for 30 seconds, being careful not to let the garlic burn. **4** Add the cabbage and spring greens; stir-fry for 3–5 minutes, until softened but not wilted. **5** Serve sprinkled with soy sauce.

NUTRIENTS PER SERVING KCAL 182 • CARBOHYDRATE 10g (of which 7g sugars) • PROTEIN 7g • FAT 13g (of which saturated fat 2g) • FIBRE 6g • SODIUM 34mg • SALT trace • VEGETABLE PORTION 2.5

BRUSSELS SPROUTS STIR-FRY

Brussels sprouts are packed with healthy vitamins, bioflavonoids and compounds believed to ward off cancer. In this quick and delicious traditional dish, they are combined with chestnuts which, unlike other nuts, are very low in fat.

175g frozen chestnuts
1 tablespoon sunflower oil
1 leek, trimmed, finely sliced and rinsed
550g Brussels sprouts, trimmed and finely sliced
225ml hot vegetable stock

Salt and black pepper

PREPARATION TIME 10 minutes
COOKING TIME 8 minutes
SERVES 4

1 Bring the chestnuts to the boil in a small saucepan of water, then cover and simmer for about 4 minutes, or until soft. Drain. **2** Heat the oil in a wok or frying pan. Add the leek and stir-fry for 30 seconds, then add the sprouts and stir-fry over a medium heat for a further 2 minutes, until the sprouts are beginning to fleck brown at the edges. **3** Add the stock, reduce the heat, cover and simmer for about 4 minutes until the sprouts are just tender but not soggy. **4** Crumble the chestnuts between your fingers and stir them into the sprouts and leeks. Cook, covered, for a further minute to heat through. Add salt and pepper to taste, then serve.

NUTRIENTS PER SERVING KCAL 160 • CARBOHYDRATE 22g (of which 8g sugars) • PROTEIN 7g • FAT 6g (of which saturated fat 1g) • FIBRE 8g • SODIUM 126mg • SALT 0.3g • VEGETABLE PORTION 2

CELERY AND APPLE

Celery is at its best in the crisp, cold days of winter when there is also a good selection of apples available. They are delicious combined with wine, herbs and capers.

1 head celery
3 red dessert apples
2–3 tablespoons olive oil
12 fresh sage leaves
1 large clove garlic
1 bay leaf

100–175ml dry white wine
2 tablespoons capers, optional
Salt and black pepper

TOTAL TIME 30 minutes
SERVES 4

1 Trim off the root end of the celery then slice the stalks into thin semicircles, cutting across the entire head. Rinse and set aside. **2** Rinse and core the apples but do not peel them. Roughly chop them into cubes and set aside. **3** Generously cover the bottom of a large frying pan with olive oil, and heat it until it shows a haze. Rinse the sage leaves, then snip them into the pan. Peel the garlic and crush it in. Allow the sage and garlic to sizzle for a few seconds, then quickly add the celery, apples and bay leaf and stir. **4** After 1 minute, pour in enough white wine to cover the mixture. Continue cooking over a high heat, stirring occasionally, until the celery is cooked but still crunchy. If the mixture dries out before the celery is cooked, add a little more wine. **5** When the celery is cooked, stir in the capers, if using, and heat them through. Season with salt and pepper to taste, remove the bay leaf from the pan and serve.

NUTRIENTS PER SERVING KCAL 141 • CARBOHYDRATE 13g (of which 12g sugars) • PROTEIN 1g • FAT 7g (of which saturated fat 1g) • FIBRE 2g • SODIUM 255mg • SALT 0.6g • VEGETABLE PORTION 1.5

ORANGE & SESAME CARROTS

The natural crunch and sweet taste of young carrots is enhanced by cooking them in orange juice. Sesame seeds provide vitamin E and calcium and a special nutty flavour.

500g small, young carrots
1 medium orange
15g butter, or 1 tablespoon sunflower oil
Salt and black pepper

1 tablespoon sesame seeds

TOTAL TIME 25 minutes
SERVES 4

1 Peel the carrots, unless they are organic – if so they will only need scrubbing. If they are very small, leave them whole; otherwise, cut them in half lengthways. **2** Wash any wax off the orange, then remove the rind with a zester and squeeze out the juice. Put the orange rind and juice into a large saucepan, then add the butter or sunflower oil and bring to the boil over a moderate heat. **3** Add the carrots to the saucepan, then season them to taste with some salt and black pepper. Bring back to the boil, then reduce the heat to moderate, cover and simmer for 10–12 minutes, shaking the pan occasionally, until the carrots are tender, but not soft. **4** Meanwhile, put the sesame seeds into a frying pan and dry fry them over a fairly high heat for about 2 minutes, shaking the pan, until they are golden. **5** Stir the sesame seeds into the carrots and serve.

NUTRIENTS PER SERVING KCAL 108 • CARBOHYDRATE 13g (of which 12g sugars) • PROTEIN 2g • FAT 6g (of which saturated fat 2g) • FIBRE 4g • SODIUM 57mg • SALT 0.14g • VEGETABLE PORTION 1

In addition to vitamin C, **Oranges** contain pectin, which may lower blood cholesterol levels.

ITALIAN BAKED CHICORY

Plump heads of chicory and the intense Mediterranean flavours of sun-dried tomatoes, lemon and black olives, taste good baked beneath a crunchy crust of cheese and breadcrumbs.

1 medium-thick slice of day-old bread or
**   15g fresh white breadcrumbs**
40g Italian-style premium cheese
6 sun-dried tomatoes in oil
4 large heads chicory, each about 150–175g
½ lemon
3 tablespoons olive oil
Black pepper
16 pitted black olives

TOTAL TIME 30 minutes
SERVES 4

1 Preheat the oven to 200°C (400°F, gas mark 6). Remove and discard the crusts from the slice of bread, if using, and turn it into breadcrumbs in a food processor. Grate the cheese into the breadcrumbs, mix them together and set aside. **2** Drain the sun-dried tomatoes on kitchen paper, then chop them and set them aside. **3** Remove any blemished outer leaves from the chicory heads, neaten the bases and cut each head into quarters lengthways. **4** Squeeze the lemon and measure out 1 tablespoon of the juice into a large, shallow, ovenproof dish. Then stir in 2 tablespoons of the olive oil. **5** Arrange the quartered chicory, cut sides up, in the ovenproof dish. Drizzle the remaining olive oil over them, then season them with black pepper. **6** Scatter the sun-dried tomatoes over the chicory, followed by the black olives, then sprinkle the cheese and breadcrumb mixture over the top. Put the dish into the oven and bake for 15 minutes, until the topping is golden brown.

NUTRIENTS PER SERVING KCAL 189 • CARBOHYDRATE 7g (of which 1g sugars) • PROTEIN 5g • FAT 16g (of which saturated fat 4g) • FIBRE 2g • SODIUM 212mg • SALT 0.5g • VEGETABLE PORTION 1

LEMON COURGETTES

This is a simple but refreshing dish of thinly sliced, tender courgettes with a generous sprinkling of finely grated lemon zest, seasoned with sea salt and black pepper.

500g small courgettes
1½ tablespoons olive oil
1 lemon
Flaky sea salt and black pepper

TOTAL TIME 15 minutes
SERVES 4

1 Trim and rinse the courgettes and slice them thinly, diagonally. **2** Heat the olive oil in a large frying pan, then add the courgettes and fry, stirring them frequently, until they are tender. **3** Meanwhile, wash any wax off the lemon and finely grate the rind. When the courgettes are cooked, sprinkle the lemon rind over them and season well with flaky sea salt and black pepper.

NUTRIENTS PER SERVING KCAL 56 • CARBOHYDRATE 2g (of which 2g sugars) • PROTEIN 2g
• FAT 4g (of which saturated fat 1g) • FIBRE 1g • SODIUM 1mg • SALT trace
• VEGETABLE PORTION 1

Courgettes contain vitamins A and C and folate. Most of the nutrients lie in the tender, edible skin.

MINTED LETTUCE, PEAS AND SPRING ONIONS

We often think of lettuce as a salad vegetable, but as this summer side dish proves, it can be delicious cooked. Fromage frais gives the rich texture of cream without the fat.

25g butter
225g shelled peas, about 675g pod weight, or frozen peas
6–8 large leaves of cos, romaine or Webb's Wonderful lettuce, rinsed and cut into large pieces
4 spring onions, trimmed and finely sliced
4–6 tablespoons vegetable stock
2 tablespoons white wine (optional)

1 teaspoon sugar
1 sprig of mint
Salt and black pepper
4 tablespoons low-fat fromage frais

PREPARATION TIME 10 minutes
COOKING TIME 15 minutes
SERVES 4

1 Melt the butter in a heavy-based saucepan over a gentle heat. Add the peas, lettuce and spring onions and cook, stirring, for about 1 minute. **2** Add the stock, wine, if using, sugar and mint sprig, with salt and black pepper to taste. **3** Bring to simmering point, then cover and simmer for 10 minutes, until the peas are tender. **4** Remove the mint and stir in the fromage frais. Serve immediately with crusty bread or as a side dish with a main meal.

NUTRIENTS PER SERVING KCAL 113 • CARBOHYDRATE 4g (of which 4g sugars) • PROTEIN 6g • FAT 6g (of which saturated fat 4g) • FIBRE 3g • SODIUM 54mg • SALT 0.1g • VEGETABLE PORTION 1

An average serving of cooked **peas** provides a quarter of the vitamin C and half the thiamin your body needs every day.

DAHL

Indian cookery uses a wide variety of lentils and split peas which are infused with flavour by simmering with spices and served as dahl – a creamy accompaniment to a vegetable curry.

350g split red lentils
1 teaspoon ground turmeric
½ teaspoon chilli powder
1cm piece fresh root ginger
2 cloves garlic
½ teaspoon garam masala
Salt
25g butter
A pinch of ground cumin
1 small onion

TOTAL TIME 25 minutes
SERVES 4

1 Put a kettle of water on to boil. Pick over the lentils and remove any small pieces of grit, then put them into a sieve and rinse them under a cold running tap. **2** Put the lentils into a saucepan and cover with 1.2 litres of boiling water from the kettle. Add the turmeric and chilli powder, cover and bring to the boil. **3** Meanwhile, peel the ginger, cut it into 4 thin slices and add them to the lentils. Peel the garlic and crush it into the saucepan. As soon as the lentils reach boiling point, reduce the heat and simmer for 10 minutes, or until they are soft and almost all the liquid has been absorbed. **4** Stir in the garam masala, then add salt to taste and cook the dahl for a further 5 minutes, leaving the pan uncovered if the mixture is still soupy. **5** Meanwhile, heat the butter and cumin in a small frying pan. Peel and dice the onion and fry it gently in the spiced butter until soft. **6** Put the dahl into a heated serving dish, stir in the fried onion and serve hot.

NUTRIENTS PER SERVING KCAL 333 • CARBOHYDRATE 51g (of which 3g sugars) • PROTEIN 21g • FAT 6g (of which saturated fat 4g) • FIBRE 4.5g • SODIUM 70mg • SALT 0.2g • VEGETABLE PORTION 1

MIXED MUSHROOMS WITH BRANDY

A harmonious mixture of dried and fresh mushrooms, cooked in olive oil and their own juices with onion, garlic, fresh parsley and a splash of brandy, makes an indulgent side dish.

A small bunch of parsley
25g dried morels or ceps
25g butter
1 tablespoon olive oil
2 cloves garlic
1 medium onion
200g button chestnut mushrooms
200g open cup mushrooms
150g oyster mushrooms
1–2 tablespoons brandy
Salt and black pepper

TOTAL TIME 30 minutes
SERVES 4

1 Put a half-filled kettle on to boil. Rinse, dry and chop enough parsley to give 3 tablespoons. Put the dried mushrooms into a small bowl, cover with 200ml of boiling water and leave to soak. **2** Meanwhile, heat the butter and olive oil in a large frying pan over a moderate heat. Peel and crush the garlic and set aside. Peel and finely chop the onion, add it to the pan and fry over a moderate heat while preparing the fresh mushrooms. **3** Clean the mushrooms. Halve the button chestnut mushrooms, slice the open cup mushrooms thickly, and cut the oyster mushrooms into strips lengthways, removing the stalks if they are tough. **4** Increase the heat under the pan, add the garlic and the mushrooms. Stir-fry for 5 minutes, until the mushrooms are just softened. **5** Meanwhile, line a sieve with kitchen paper and place it over a bowl. Pour the soaked mushrooms into it, so that the paper catches any grit and the soaking water drains into the bowl. Reserve this liquid. Rinse and chop the drained mushrooms. **6** With a slotted spoon, lift the fried onions and mushrooms from the frying pan and put them into a bowl, leaving their juices in the pan. **7** Add the drained mushrooms and their soaking water to the pan. Boil rapidly until the liquid has a syrupy consistency. **8** Stir in the brandy. Return the mushrooms to the pan, season to taste, stir in the parsley and reheat. Transfer to a warm dish to serve.

NUTRIENTS PER SERVING KCAL 126 • **CARBOHYDRATE 4g (of which 3g sugars)** • **PROTEIN 5g** • **FAT 9g (of which saturated fat 4g)** • **FIBRE 2g** • **SODIUM 46mg** • **SALT 0.1g** • **VEGETABLE PORTION 1**

HONEY-ROAST PARSNIPS, SQUASH AND POTATOES

Roasting retains the nutrients and colour, of a variety of winter vegetables, enhanced by the addition of a sweet honey glaze sharpened with grainy mustard.

2 parsnips, peeled

1 small winter squash, such as acorn, pumpkin or onion squash

2 large potatoes, cut into wedges

1 tablespoon sunflower oil

2 tablespoons honey

2 teaspoons wholegrain mustard

1 tablespoon lemon juice

PREPARATION TIME 20 minutes

COOKING TIME 50 minutes

SERVES 4

1 Heat the oven to 200°C (400°F, gas mark 6). Halve or quarter the parsnips and remove the woody core, then cut into chunks. **2** Halve the squash and remove the seeds. Cut into wedges and peel. **3** Cook the parsnips, squash and potatoes in boiling, salted water for 2 minutes, until slightly tender. Drain well. **4** Put the oil in a shallow ovenproof dish and heat in the oven for 2–3 minutes. Add the drained vegetables, turning them to coat them in oil. Bake for about 30 minutes until they start to look golden, turning them halfway through the cooking time. **5** Meanwhile, mix the honey with the mustard and lemon juice. When the vegetables are beginning to brown, remove them from the oven and pour the honey and mustard mixture over them. Stir to coat. **6** Return the vegetables to the oven and continue cooking for 10-15 minutes until they are deeply golden. Serve hot with the main meal.

NUTRIENTS PER SERVING KCAL 220 • **CARBOHYDRATE 44g (of which 22g sugars)** • **PROTEIN 5g** • **FAT 4g (of which saturated fat 0.5g)** • **FIBRE 6g** • **SODIUM 21mg** • **SALT trace** • **VEGETABLE PORTION 2**

Pumpkins and the many varieties of winter squash, such as **acorn** and **butternut**, are particularly important in a vegetarian diet where there are no animal proteins to provide vitamin A.

POTATO AND GREEN BEAN CURRY

Tender, sliced new potatoes and fine green beans are cooked in an aromatic mixture of butter and delicate spices. Serve with rice or naan bread, or as a side dish to another curry.

500g small new potatoes
250g fine green beans
15g butter
3 tablespoons sunflower oil
2 small green chillies
½ teaspoon cumin seeds
½ teaspoon ground turmeric

¼ teaspoon garam masala
1 clove garlic
Salt

TOTAL TIME 30 minutes
SERVES 4

1 Scrub the new potatoes and cut them into thick slices. Top and tail the green beans, then cut them into 2.5cm lengths, rinse them and leave them to drain. **2** Heat the butter and oil in a wide, shallow saucepan or frying pan, over a high heat. When they begin to sizzle, stir in the whole green chillies and the cumin seeds, turmeric and garam masala. Peel the garlic and crush it into the pan; stir and fry for 30 seconds. **3** Add the potatoes to the pan and season with some salt. Stir them until they are coated with the spiced butter and oil. **4** Stir in the beans, cover the pan, then reduce the heat to moderate and cook for 15 minutes, stirring occasionally. The curry is ready as soon as the potatoes are tender.

NUTRIENTS PER SERVING KCAL 197 • CARBOHYDRATE 20g (of which 3g sugars) • PROTEIN 3g • FAT 12g (of which saturated fat 3g) • FIBRE 2.5g • SODIUM 36mg • SALT trace • VEGETABLE PORTION 0

POTATOES BOULANGÈRE

Slow-baked potato dishes are tender and flavourful. This version is made with stock instead of the usual cream and cheese, making it healthier but without losing any of the taste.

750g floury potatoes, such as King Edwards, peeled
225g onions, thinly sliced
Salt and black pepper
Freshly grated nutmeg
1–2 cloves garlic, crushed
600ml vegetable stock

1 tablespoon low-fat spread

PREPARATION TIME 15 minutes, plus 15 minutes soaking and 5 minutes standing
COOKING TIME 1 hour 30 minutes
SERVES 4-6

1 Slice the potatoes by putting them through the thin blade of a food processor or use a sharp knife. Put them in a bowl with the onions, cover with cold water and leave to soak for 15 minutes to remove some of the starch and soften the onions. **2** Heat the oven to 180°C (350°F, gas mark 4). Drain the potatoes and onions and pat them dry with kitchen paper. Arrange a layer of onions and potatoes in the base of a shallow ovenproof serving dish. Season with salt, pepper and nutmeg to taste, then repeat to make four or five layers in total, ending with the seasonings. **3** Stir the garlic into the stock, then pour it over the vegetables. Dot the top with the low-fat spread. Bake for 1½ hours, or until the top is browned and the potatoes feel soft when they are pierced with a skewer. Leave the dish to stand for 5 minutes before serving.

NUTRIENTS PER SERVING KCAL 161 • CARBOHYDRATE 31g (of which 5g sugars) • PROTEIN 4g • FAT 4g (of which saturated fat 1g) • FIBRE 4g • SODIUM 98mg • SALT 0.25g • VEGETABLE PORTION 0

Potatoes are a healthy high-carbohydrate food that also contains protein and fibre.

Best potatoes for:
Chips – Maris Piper
Jacket – Desirée
Mash – King Edward or Maris Piper
Roast – King Edward or Desirée
Salads – Jersey Royals.

HOT CAJUN POTATO WEDGES

Easy-to-make spicy wedges make a tasty side dish or a flavour-packed snack.

1kg large potatoes
1½ teaspoons sunflower oil
2 tablespoons fresh wholemeal breadcrumbs
A pinch of cayenne pepper
½ teaspoon ground cumin
1 teaspoon garlic salt
1 teaspoon paprika

1 teaspoon ground black pepper
1 teaspoon dried thyme

PREPARATION TIME 5 minutes
COOKING TIME 35–40 minutes
SERVES 4–6

1 Heat the oven to 220°C (425°F, gas mark 7). Scrub the potatoes, leaving the skins on, and cut each one lengthways into eight wedges. Place them in a large mixing bowl, add the oil and toss to coat the wedges thinly and evenly. **2** Mix together the breadcrumbs, cayenne pepper, cumin, garlic salt, paprika, pepper and thyme in a large bowl. Add the potatoes and toss until they are evenly coated. **3** Arrange the wedges in a single layer on a large nonstick baking sheet and bake for 35–40 minutes until they are golden brown and crisp. Serve them hot with some low-fat Greek yoghurt as a dip.

NUTRIENTS PER SERVING KCAL 227 • CARBOHYDRATE 49g (of which 1.5g sugars) • PROTEIN 6g • FAT 2g (no saturated fat) • FIBRE 4g • SODIUM 58mg • SALT 0.14g • VEGETABLE PORTION 0

SWEET ROASTED SQUASH WITH SHALLOTS

Roasted vegetables are sweetened and slightly caramelised with a touch of maple syrup or honey.

900g butternut squash
8 shallots
A few sprigs of fresh thyme
1 teaspoon olive oil
2 teaspoons maple syrup or clear honey

Salt and black pepper

PREPARATION TIME 15 minutes
COOKING TIME 30–35 minutes
SERVES 4

1 Heat the oven to 190°C (375°F, gas mark 5). Cut the squash in half lengthways, remove the seeds and peel, then cut the flesh into 3cm cubes. Put them into a large mixing bowl. **2** Peel the shallots and add them to the squash with most of the sprigs of thyme, reserving a few to use as a garnish. **3** Mix together the oil and maple syrup or honey and add salt and pepper to taste, then pour it into the vegetables, tossing to coat them evenly. **4** Tip the vegetables into a roasting tin and cook for 30–35 minutes, turning them occasionally, until they are tender and golden brown. Garnish with the reserved sprigs of thyme and serve as an accompaniment to a main dish.

NUTRIENTS PER SERVING KCAL 112 • CARBOHYDRATE 24g (of which 14g sugars) • PROTEIN 3g • FAT 13g (of which saturated fat 3g) • FIBRE 4g • SODIUM 11mg • SALT trace • VEGETABLE PORTION 3

The flavour of **honey** depends on which flowers the bees have visited – mild acacia honey is particularly suitable for cooking.

LEMON-BRAISED SPINACH WITH MUSHROOMS AND CROUTONS

This swift and delicious way to serve spinach is enlivened with soy sauce and crunchy croutons.

400g spinach
½ lemon
200g oyster mushrooms, thinly sliced
2 teaspoons soy sauce
3 spring onions, thinly sliced
Black pepper

FOR THE CROUTONS
2 thin slices wholemeal bread, crusts removed
½ teaspoon garlic purée, or crushed garlic
Tabasco sauce, to taste

PREPARATION TIME 10 minutes
COOKING TIME 5–10 minutes
SERVES 4

1 Heat the grill to medium. Rinse the spinach, remove any tough stems and drain well. **2** To make the croutons, cut the bread into small dice. Mix the garlic purée or crushed garlic and Tabasco sauce together in a bowl, then stir in the bread. Transfer the spiced bread to a baking sheet or grill pan in a single layer and grill for 1–2 minutes, turning the dice over occasionally, until the croutons are golden brown. Set aside. **3** Remove a few strips of lemon zest and reserve, then squeeze the juice. Put the lemon juice, mushrooms, soy sauce and spring onions in a saucepan over a medium-high heat and cook, shaking the pan occasionally, for 2–3 minutes until the vegetables have softened. **4** Turn the heat to high, add the spinach and stir for 2 minutes, or until the spinach has wilted and most of the juices have evaporated. Season with pepper. Serve the spinach hot, with the croutons and reserved lemon zest scattered over the top.

NUTRIENTS PER SERVING KCAL 55 • CARBOHYDRATE 7g (of which 2g sugars) • PROTEIN 4g • FAT 1g (no saturated fat) • FIBRE 3g • SODIUM 430mg • SALT 1g • VEGETABLE PORTION 1

BABY VEGETABLES WITH SOURED CREAM

A rich, warm trio of crisp steamed vegetables makes an excellent accompaniment to a main dish, but it can also hold its own as a vegetable salad, served with hot, crusty bread.

175g baby carrots
250g baby courgettes
250g fine asparagus spears
200ml soured cream
2 teaspoons wholegrain mustard

15g salted butter, at room temperature
Black pepper

TOTAL TIME 20 minutes
SERVES 4

1 Prepare a steamer by half filling the bottom pan with water and putting it on to boil.
2 Meanwhile, peel and trim the carrots and cut any large ones in half lengthways. Trim and rinse the baby courgettes and halve them lengthways, then trim and rinse the asparagus spears.
3 Put the carrots into the steamer, cover them and steam for 5 minutes. Then lay the courgettes over the carrots, and the asparagus over the courgettes. Replace the cover, and steam for a further 5 minutes. **4** While the vegetables are in the steamer, put the soured cream into a saucepan, then stir in the mustard and heat the mixture very gently until just warmed through. **5** Warm a serving bowl, put the vegetables into it and stir in the butter and some black pepper. Pour in the warm cream dressing, stir gently to mix it in thoroughly, and serve at once.

NUTRIENTS PER SERVING KCAL 170 • CARBOHYDRATE 7g (of which 6g sugars) • PROTEIN 5g • FAT 14g (of which saturated fat 8g) • FIBRE 3g • SODIUM 55mg • SALT 0.14g • VEGETABLE PORTION 2

veg

tables
as a main course

VEGETABLES
AS A MAIN COURSE

CELERIAC DUMPLINGS IN TOMATO BROTH

Fluffy white dumplings in a light tomato and vegetable broth make a delicious lunch or supper. Both the soup and dumplings can be made in advance, ready to be simmered just before serving.

1 red pepper
1 tablespoon extra virgin olive oil
1 leek, thinly sliced
1 garlic clove, crushed
900ml vegetable stock, preferably home-made
1 tablespoon tomato purée
140g frozen petit pois
2 tomatoes, about 100g in total, skinned and roughly chopped
salt and pepper
sprigs of fresh basil to garnish

CELERIAC DUMPLINGS
150g celeriac, diced, or 55g cooked celeriac, mashed
75g fine fresh white breadcrumbs
125g soft mild goat's cheese
2 teaspoons chopped fresh basil
1 egg, beaten

PREPARATION TIME about 1 hour, plus about 15 minutes cooling
COOKING TIME about 20 minutes
SERVES 4

1 Preheat the grill to the hottest setting, then grill the red pepper for about 10 minutes, turning it often, until the skin is charred all over. Put it in a polythene bag and set it aside until cool enough to handle. Peel the pepper, discard the seeds and cut the flesh into 1cm squares. **2** For the dumplings, cook the diced celeriac in boiling water for 10–15 minutes or until very tender. Drain well, then purée in a blender or food processor, or mash until smooth. Set aside to cool. **3** Meanwhile, heat the oil in a large saucepan. Add the leek and garlic, and cook for 1 minute. Stir in the red pepper, stock and tomato purée. Bring to the boil, then reduce the heat and simmer for 8 minutes. Add the peas halfway through the cooking. Remove from the heat. Stir in the tomatoes and seasoning to taste, then set aside. **4** Add the breadcrumbs, goat's cheese, basil and egg to the celeriac, with seasoning to taste. Mix well until all the ingredients are thoroughly combined. Use 2 small spoons (teaspoons are suitable) to shape the mixture into 12 small dumplings, setting them on a plate as they are made. **5** Bring a large saucepan of water to the boil. Gently lower half the dumplings, one by one, into the water on a draining spoon. Bring the water back to the boil, then cover, reduce the heat and simmer gently for 4–5 minutes. Use the draining spoon to remove the dumplings from the pan to a double layer of kitchen paper to drain. Repeat with the remaining dumplings. **6** Return the tomato broth to the heat and bring to the boil. Ladle the soup into bowls, add the dumplings and garnish with basil. Serve immediately.

NUTRIENTS PER SERVING KCAL 225 • CARBOHYDRATE 22g (of which 7g sugars) • PROTEIN 12g • FAT 10g (of which saturated fat 4g) • FIBRE 3g • SODIUM 512mg • SALT 1.3g • VEGETABLE PORTION 1

TOMATOES WITH A SPINACH STUFFING

A generous filling of fresh spinach enriched with pine kernels and tangy cheese gives an Italian flavour to the giant tomatoes in this dish, and it is equally delicious served hot or cold.

1½ tablespoons olive oil
250g fresh spinach
4 large tomatoes, about 225g each
125g pine kernels
1 clove garlic
125g Italian-style premium cheese
Salt and black pepper

TOTAL TIME 30 minutes
SERVES 2

1 Preheat the oven to 220°C (425°F, gas mark 7). Lightly oil a baking sheet. Remove the stalks, rinse and dry the spinach. **2** Heat the rest of the oil in a saucepan and add the spinach, cover and cook for 2 minutes. Uncover, stir, and leave to cook for 1 minute. Drain off the liquid, transfer the spinach to a bowl and set it aside. **3** Rinse and dry the tomatoes; slice off and reserve the tops. Discard the pith, seeds and juice from the centre of each. **4** Lightly toast the pine kernels, then add them to the spinach. Peel the garlic and crush it in, then grate over the Parmesan, season to taste with salt and black pepper and mix. **5** Press the spinach mixture into the tomatoes, piling it up, then replace the tops, balancing them on the stuffing and bake them on the top shelf of the oven for 12–15 minutes.

NUTRIENTS PER SERVING KCAL 790 • CARBOHYDRATE 9g (of which 8g sugars) • PROTEIN 36g • FAT 68g (of which saturated fat 16g) • FIBRE 5g • SODIUM 658mg • SALT 1.6g • VEGETABLE PORTION 2

Dishes where **lime** juice has
been used as a flavouring
need little salt – which can be
helpful if you are trying to follow
a low-sodium diet.

MARINATED TOFU AND MANGO KEBABS WITH GREEN MANGO SALSA

Protein-rich tofu comes alive with a Thai salsa flavoured with chilli, coconut cream and lime.

500g fresh tofu
1 large ripe mango, peeled and cubed

FOR THE MARINADE
1–2 fresh red chillies, deseeded and chopped
2 cloves garlic, crushed
1 tablespoon grated ginger
1 tablespoon clear honey
Grated zest and juice of 1 lime
3 tablespoons dry sherry
2 tablespoons dark soy sauce

FOR THE SALSA
3 tablespoons coconut cream

Juice of ½ lime
1 large green unripe mango, peeled and coarsely grated
Salt

TO GARNISH lemon wedges and sliced spring onions

PREPARATION TIME 15 minutes, plus 30 minutes draining and 30 minutes marinating
COOKING TIME 6–8 minutes
SERVES 4

1 Cover a large plate with several layers of kitchen paper. Arrange the tofu on top and cover with more paper, then put a plate on top and weigh it down with a can. Allow the tofu to drain for 30 minutes, then pour off the liquid and cut the tofu into 2.5cm cubes. **2** To make the marinade, combine all the ingredients in a shallow bowl. Add the tofu to the bowl and marinate for at least 30 minutes, stirring and turning a few times. **3** Meanwhile, make the salsa. Mix all the ingredients together with salt to taste in a small bowl and set aside. Heat the grill or light the barbecue. **4** Lift the tofu out of the marinade and thread it onto skewers alternately with the mango pieces. Add the remaining marinade to the salsa. **5** Grill the kebabs for 6–8 minutes, turning them once or twice, until the tofu is browned and heated through. Serve hot with the salsa, garnished with the strips of spring onions, and lime wedges.

NUTRIENTS PER SERVING KCAL 230 • CARBOHYDRATE 17g (of which 14g sugars) • PROTEIN 16g • FAT 10g (of which saturated fat 6g) • FIBRE 2g • SODIUM 537mg • SALT 1.3g • VEGETABLE PORTION 1

BABY VEGETABLE FRICASSÉE

Tender poached vegetables are served in a herby béchamel sauce and given a crunchy cheese topping. They are delicious served with tagliatelle or boiled new potatoes.

750g mixture of young and baby vegetables such as broccoli, carrots, cauliflower, fennel, leeks, mushrooms, onions, patty pan squash or courgettes, and red or yellow peppers
2 tablespoons dry vermouth
1 bay leaf
2–3 fresh parsley stalks
1 sprig fresh thyme
Salt and black pepper
25g Parmesan cheese, grated
2 tablespoons wholemeal breadcrumbs

FOR THE BÉCHAMEL SAUCE:
50g low-fat spread
3 tablespoons plain white flour
150ml semi-skimmed milk
3 tablespoons half-fat crème fraîche
2 tablespoons coarsely chopped fresh parsley or marjoram

PREPARATION TIME 15 minutes
COOKING TIME 30–35 minutes
SERVES 4

1 Prepare your chosen vegetables: trim broccoli or cauliflower into small florets; top and tail carrots; top, tail and chop fennel finely; slice leeks thickly; slice mushrooms; cut onions into quarters; halve patty pan squash or top and tail baby courgettes; and cut peppers into squares. **2** Put 600ml of water into a large saucepan and add the vermouth, bay leaf, parsley stalks, thyme, salt and pepper, then bring to the boil. Add the vegetables, reduce the heat and simmer for 5 minutes. **3** Using a slotted spoon, transfer the vegetables to a shallow 1.5 litre flameproof dish. Set aside and keep warm. **4** Discard the herbs and return the vegetable stock to a fast boil. Cook, uncovered, for 10 minutes, or until it is reduced by half. Heat the grill to a medium heat. **5** To make the sauce, melt the fat spread in a large saucepan and whisk in the flour. Cook for 1–2 seconds, then gradually strain in the stock, add the milk and whisk. Bring to the boil, reduce the heat and simmer for 3 minutes. Remove from the heat, stir in the crème fraîche and chopped herb and season to taste. **6** Pour the sauce over the vegetables, sprinkle the cheese and breadcrumbs over the top, and place under the grill for 2–3 minutes until the topping is lightly browned, then serve.

NUTRIENTS PER SERVING KCAL 279 • CARBOHYDRATE 28g (of which 9g sugars) • PROTEIN 9g • FAT 15g (of which saturated fat 5g) • FIBRE 4g • SODIUM 146mg • SALT 0.4g • VEGETABLE PORTION 2

ASPARAGUS PIPERADE

In this well-travelled Spanish dish, fresh asparagus, sweet peppers, chunks of chopped tomatoes and just enough chilli to tantalise the palate are temptingly combined with fluffy scrambled eggs.

1 large onion
1 green chilli
1 large red pepper
1 large green pepper
3 tablespoons olive oil
3 cloves garlic
Salt and black pepper
500g asparagus
400g canned chopped tomatoes
8 slices of bread, or 4 crumpets or muffins
Butter for spreading
4 large eggs

TIME 30 minutes
SERVES 4

1 Peel the onion and slice it; rinse, deseed and dice the chilli, then rinse, deseed and slice the peppers. **2** Heat the olive oil in a large frying pan or a wok with a lid. Peel the garlic, crush it into the oil and add the onion, diced chilli and peppers, with salt and pepper to taste. Stir-fry them for 1 minute, then cover and cook over a high heat for 3–4 minutes, shaking the pan occasionally. **3** Trim the woody ends from the asparagus and rinse them, then cut each of the spears into four pieces. Add the asparagus to the onions, then cover the pan and leave them to cook for about 7–8 minutes, stirring them occasionally. Preheat the grill to high. **4** Stir the canned tomatoes into the vegetables, increase the heat and bring the mixture to simmering point, then let it cook, uncovered, for 2 minutes. **5** Meanwhile, toast the bread or split and toast the crumpets or muffins, and butter them. **6** Break the eggs into a bowl and beat them lightly, then add them to the vegetables and scramble them over a moderate heat, stirring, until the eggs are just set. **7** Serve surrounded by buttered toast, crumpets or muffins.

NUTRIENTS PER SERVING KCAL 470 • CARBOHYDRATE 47g (of which 13g sugars) • PROTEIN 20g • FAT 23g (of which saturated fat 7g) • FIBRE 5g • SODIUM 544mg • SALT 1.3g • VEGETABLE PORTION 4

Tofu is high in protein, very low in saturated fats and cholesterol free — an ideal ingredient in a balanced vegetarian diet.

CHINESE-STYLE TOFU OMELETTES

A sweet sauce blends delicate rice wine with hoisin, garlic and green peas in this traditional Oriental omelette. If you can't buy silken tofu, use plain tofu, which is slightly firmer and drier.

600g silken tofu, firm or soft
3 eggs
3–4 spring onions, chopped
Salt and black pepper
2 tablespoons oil

FOR THE SAUCE
175ml vegetable stock

2 tablespoons hoisin sauce
2 tablespoons Chinese rice wine, or dry sherry
I clove garlic, crushed
150g peas, defrosted if frozen

PREPARATION TIME 10 minutes
COOKING TIME 30–35 minutes
SERVES 4

1 Heat the oven to low to keep the omelettes warm. **2** Mash the tofu with a fork in a large bowl until it is thoroughly broken down, then beat in the eggs and spring onions and season generously with salt and pepper. **3** Heat ½ tablespoon of the oil in a large nonstick frying pan until it is very hot. Add a quarter of the tofu mixture to the pan to make two omelettes at a time, keeping them well apart. Fry them for 3–4 minutes on each side until they have turned golden brown, turning them carefully because the mixture breaks up easily. **4** Transfer the omelettes to a heatproof plate as they are made and put them in the oven to keep warm. Repeat the process three more times, adding oil to the pan as necessary, to make eight omelettes in total. **5** After all the omelettes have been made, add the vegetable stock to the pan and scrape up any caramelised cooking juices on the base, then bring the liquid to the boil. Stir in the hoisin sauce, Chinese rice wine or sherry, garlic and peas and let them simmer for 2–3 minutes until the sauce has thickened slightly and the flavours have combined. Adjust the seasoning to taste. **6** Lay two omelettes on each plate, pour the sauce over them and serve while they are still hot.

NUTRIENTS PER SERVING KCAL 304 • CARBOHYDRATE 9g (of which 2g sugars) • PROTEIN 26g • FAT 18g (of which saturated fat 5g) • FIBRE 2g • SODIUM 400mg • SALT 1g • VEGETABLE PORTION 0

TOFU STIR-FRY WITH CASHEWS

Soft tofu soaks up the flavour of a tangy, Oriental-style marinade of soy sauce and dry sherry. It is then stir-fried with a crisp mixture of vegetables and cashew nuts and served with noodles.

280g tofu (fresh or packeted)
1cm piece fresh root ginger
150g sugarsnap peas
100g fresh shiitake mushrooms
1 large red or yellow pepper
400g Chinese cabbage or cos lettuce
1 bunch of spring onions
3 tablespoons groundnut oil
250g thread egg noodles
Salt
85g roasted cashew nuts

FOR THE MARINADE
2 cloves garlic
1½ tablespoons Japanese soy sauce
2 tablespoons dry sherry
1½ teaspoons toasted sesame oil
1 teaspoon brown sugar
Black pepper

TOTAL TIME 30 minutes
SERVES 4

1 Preheat the oven to a low setting and boil a kettle of water. To make the marinade, peel the garlic and crush it into a bowl. Add the soy sauce, sherry, sesame oil, sugar and pepper and stir. **2** Drain the tofu and cut it into oblongs 1cm thick, add it to the marinade and leave it to soak. **3** Peel and finely chop the ginger. Rinse, top and tail the sugarsnap peas. Clean the mushrooms and slice them thinly. Rinse, quarter and deseed the pepper, stack the pieces and slice them into long strips. Set them all aside. **4** Remove any damaged outer leaves from the cabbage or lettuce, then rinse, dry and cut it across into 1cm slices. Trim, rinse and slice the spring onions. **5** Heat 1 tablespoon of groundnut oil in a frying pan over a moderate heat. Drain the tofu, reserving the marinade, stir-fry it for 3 minutes, then remove and keep warm. **6** Heat the remaining oil in the pan. Add the ginger, sugarsnap peas and mushrooms and stir-fry them for 2 minutes. Then add the sliced pepper, stir-fry for 2 minutes more, and add the cabbage or lettuce and the spring onions and stir-fry for a further 2 minutes. **7** Put the noodles into a bowl, add salt and cover with boiling water. Stir gently, cover and set aside for as long as instructed on the packet. **8** While the noodles are cooking, pour the reserved marinade into the vegetables, add the roasted cashew nuts and stir for 1–2 minutes until the marinade is hot. **9** Stir the tofu into the vegetables and keep warm. Drain the noodles. Serve mixed with the vegetables.

NUTRIENTS PER SERVING KCAL 574 • CARBOHYDRATE 58g (of which 10g sugars) • PROTEIN 24g • FAT 30g (of which saturated fat 7g) • FIBRE 7g • SODIUM 400mg • SALT 1g • VEGETABLE PORTION 2

SPICED CARROT AND CHICKPEA FRITTERS

These vivid, healthy carrot and chickpea patties are whizzed together in a food processor with fresh herbs and strong spices to produce a fresh-tasting variation on the vegeburger.

350g carrots
1 clove garlic
A large bunch of fresh coriander
400g canned chickpeas
1½ teaspoons ground cumin
1½ teaspoons ground coriander
1 large egg
2 tablespoons plain flour
Oil for frying

TO SERVE hamburger buns, or baps, and salad

TOTAL TIME 20 minutes
SERVES 4

1 Peel the carrots, grate them coarsely and set them aside. **2** Peel and roughly chop the garlic, then rinse, dry and chop enough coriander to give 6 tablespoons. **3** Drain and rinse the chickpeas and put them into a food processor with the garlic, coriander and both ground spices. Process to a rough paste then add the carrot, egg and flour and process briefly until evenly mixed but slightly rugged. **4** Heat the oil in a frying pan and divide the mixture into 8 fritters. Fry in batches for 2–3 minutes on each side, until golden, then drain on kitchen paper. Serve in buns or baps, with salad. If necessary, you can make the fritters in advance and fry them later.

NUTRIENTS PER SERVING KCAL 223 • **CARBOHYDRATE 25g (of which 7g sugars)** • **PROTEIN 9g**
• **FAT 10g (of which saturated fat 2g)** • **FIBRE 6g** • **SODIUM 223mg** • **SALT 0.5g**
• **VEGETABLE PORTION 1**

SPINACH AND CELERIAC ROULADE

Celeriac has a mild celery-like flavour and an appealing crunchy texture. Combined with spinach, crème fraîche and a touch of Cheddar, it makes an elegant roulade.

350g fresh spinach, washed and tough stalks removed
15g butter
3 tablespoons half-fat crème fraîche
4 eggs, separated
25g mature Cheddar cheese, grated
Salt and black pepper

FOR THE FILLING
225g celeriac, peeled and finely grated
1 tablespoon lemon juice
4 tablespoons low-fat fromage frais
2 tablespoons reduced-fat mayonnaise

PREPARATION TIME 30 minutes
COOKING TIME 15 minutes
SERVES 4

1 Heat the oven to 190°C (375°F, gas mark 5). Line a 33 x 23cm swiss roll tin with baking parchment. Put the spinach into a large saucepan, cover tightly and cook over a moderate heat for a few minutes, shaking the pan occasionally, until wilted. Drain well, then chop finely. **2** Heat the butter in a small saucepan and add the chopped spinach. Cook gently until any excess liquid has evaporated. Remove from the heat and leave to cool. **3** Add the crème fraîche, egg yolks and cheese to the spinach, with salt and pepper to taste. In a clean bowl, whisk the egg whites until stiff, then fold them into the spinach and egg mixture. Spoon into the prepared tin and smooth the surface, using a palette knife. **4** Bake for 10–15 minutes until firm to the touch and golden. Turn out onto a sheet of greaseproof paper and peel away the lining paper. While still warm, carefully roll up the roulade in the greaseproof paper and place it seam side down on a cooling rack. **5** Meanwhile, to make the filling, put the celeriac into a bowl and sprinkle with lemon juice. Add the fromage frais, mayonnaise and some salt and pepper and mix well. **6** Unroll the roulade, remove the greaseproof paper and spread with the celeriac mixture. Roll up again and transfer the roulade carefully to a serving dish. Serve warm or chilled. If not serving the roulade immediately, let it come to room temperature about 30 minutes before serving.

NUTRIENTS PER SERVING KCAL 250 • CARBOHYDRATE 5g (of which 4g sugars) • PROTEIN 14g • FAT 16g (of which saturated fat 6g) • FIBRE 4g • SODIUM 407mg • SALT 1g • VEGETABLE PORTION 1

If you don't enjoy the soggy texture of cooked **spinach**, try it as a salad vegetable instead. It's rich in vitamin C, potassium, folate and vitamin K.

BLACK BEAN CHILLI

The rich, smoky flavour of this dish goes well with a herbed rice – try lemon, garlic and dill in it.

500g black beans
1 bay leaf
2 tablespoons cumin seeds
2 tablespoons dried oregano
½ teaspoon cayenne pepper
1–2 tablespoons chilli powder
1 tablespoon paprika
2 tablespoons sunflower oil
350g onions, chopped
6 cloves garlic, chopped
400g canned chopped tomatoes

½ teaspoon Liquid Smoke (optional)
Salt
2 tablespoons red wine vinegar

TO GARNISH chopped fresh coriander

PREPARATION TIME 15 minutes, plus overnight soaking
COOKING TIME 1½–2½ hours
SERVES 8 as part of a buffet

1 Soak the beans overnight in water to cover. Next day, drain them, cover with fresh water, bring to the boil and cook for 15 minutes. Drain again, add 1.2 litres of fresh water and the bay leaf and bring to the boil, then simmer for 20 minutes. **2** Meanwhile, heat a small, heavy-based frying pan. Add the cumin seeds; when they begin to darken, add the oregano and stir for 10 seconds. Take the pan off the heat, stir in the cayenne pepper, chilli powder and paprika, then crush to a powder with a pestle and mortar. **3** Heat the oil in a frying pan over a medium heat and cook the onions for 5 minutes. Add the garlic and fry for 1 minute, then add the spices and cook for a further 2 minutes, stirring. **4** Add the tomatoes with their juice and the Liquid Smoke, if using, and cook the sauce over a medium heat for 2 minutes. **5** Pour the spiced tomato sauce into the beans and simmer for 30 minutes to 1 hour 30 minutes, depending on the age of the beans (older beans take longer to cook), until they are thoroughly soft, but not breaking apart. Add more water during cooking if necessary and stir occasionally to ensure they do not burn on the base. Add salt and extra cayenne to taste. **6** Just before serving, stir in the vinegar and garnish with chopped coriander. Tip: Liquid Smoke, available in some supermarkets, adds an unusual, smoky overtone to food, but use it sparingly.

NUTRIENTS PER SERVING KCAL 490 • CARBOHYDRATE 77g (of which 11g sugars) • PROTEIN 31g • FAT 8g (of which saturated fat 1.5g) • FIBRE 12g • SODIUM 62mg • SALT 0.15g • VEGETABLE PORTION 1

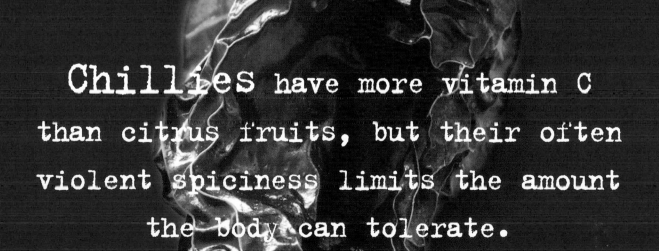

Chillies have more vitamin C than citrus fruits, but their often violent spiciness limits the amount the body can tolerate.

BEAN AND MUSHROOM BURGERS

Tuck into these hearty, lightly spiced vegetarian burgers, made with red kidney beans and red onions and served with pitta bread, salad and a sweet red onion relish.

400g canned red kidney beans
2 medium red onions, about 200g in total
4 tablespoons olive oil
2 tablespoons red wine vinegar
2 tablespoons light muscovado sugar
200g cup mushrooms
1 clove garlic
1 tablespoon garam masala
2 tablespoons wholemeal flour
A small bunch of fresh mint
Salt and black pepper

TO SERVE 4 pitta breads

TOTAL TIME 30 Minutes
SERVES 4

1 Rinse the beans well and spread them out on a tea towel to drain. Peel the onions. **2** To make the red onion relish, heat 1 tablespoon of olive oil in a saucepan. Slice one of the onions thinly and add it to the pan with the vinegar and sugar. Bring to the boil, stirring, then reduce the heat and leave it to simmer, uncovered, for 15–20 minutes, or until the onion is softened and slightly sticky, stirring it from time to time. Then remove the pan from the heat and keep it warm. **3** Meanwhile, quarter the other onion and put it into a food processor. Clean the mushrooms, add them to the onion and process until finely chopped. Alternatively, chop them both finely by hand. **4** Heat another tablespoon of olive oil in a frying pan, add the onion and mushroom mixture and cook over a fairly high heat, stirring occasionally, for 5–8 minutes, or until golden and dry. **5** Peel the garlic, crush it into the mushroom mixture, stir in the garam masala and flour and cook for 1 minute. Rinse, dry and chop enough mint to give 2 tablespoons. Remove the pan from the heat, add the mint and season well with salt and pepper. **6** Put the kidney beans onto a deep plate and mash them firmly with a potato masher, then stir in the cooled mushroom mixture. **7** Divide the mixture into four and, with lightly floured hands, shape each portion into a burger. **8** Heat the remaining oil in a large frying pan, add the beanburgers and cook them over a fairly high heat for 6–8 minutes, turning them once, until they are well browned. Warm the pitta breads. **9** Arrange the burgers on a warm dish or individual plates and spoon the onion relish over the top of them. Serve with the warm pittas and a green salad.

NUTRIENTS PER SERVING KCAL 461 • **CARBOHYDRATE 73g (of which 15g sugars)** • **PROTEIN 15g** • **FAT 13g (of which saturated fat 2g)** • **FIBRE 9g** • **SODIUM 665mg** • **SALT 1.6g** • **VEGETABLE PORTION 1**

Parsnips are at their sweetest a few weeks after the first frost, when their starch starts turning to sugar.

VEGETABLE HOTPOT WITH DUMPLINGS

Casseroles and hotpots are a popular winter staple, when hearty root vegetables provide warming, sustaining nourishment; they're even better with dumplings.

1 tablespoon olive oil
15g butter
225g baby or pickling onions, peeled
2 carrots, cut into wedges
1 small parsnip, peeled and cut into chunks
1 small swede, peeled and cut into chunks
350g potatoes, peeled and halved or quartered
225g frozen chestnuts
400ml vegetable stock
1 sprig of fresh thyme
175g green beans

Salt and black pepper

FOR THE DUMPLINGS
175g self-raising flour
2 tablespoons chopped fresh parsley
85g butter

PREPARATION TIME 30 minutes
COOKING TIME 1¼ hours
SERVES 4

1 Heat the oil and butter in a large flameproof casserole and fry the onions for 2–3 minutes until just beginning to brown. **2** Add the carrots, parsnip and swede and stir-fry gently over a low heat for 2–3 minutes. Cover and cook over a low heat for 6–8 minutes. **3** Add the potatoes, chestnuts, stock and thyme. Add salt and pepper, then cover the casserole and cook over a very gentle heat for 30–40 minutes. Meanwhile, prepare the green beans. If using runner beans, top and tail and string if necessary. Slice thinly using a sharp knife or runner bean slicer. For green beans top and tail. Add the beans to the stew and cook for a further 5 minutes. **4** To make the dumplings, put the flour and parsley into a bowl. Add a pinch of salt and rub in the butter. Stir in enough water to make a soft dough, then shape the dough into eight small dumplings. **5** Arrange the dumplings on top of the vegetables. Cover tightly and cook gently for a further 10–15 minutes until the dumplings are well risen and fluffy. Serve at once.

NUTRIENTS PER SERVING KCAL 600 • CARBOHYDRATE 86g (of which 18g sugars) • PROTEIN 11g
• FAT 26g (of which saturated fat 14g) • FIBRE 10g • SODIUM 400mg • SALT 1g
• VEGETABLE PORTION 2

AUBERGINE ROLLS

Unlike many aubergine recipes which swim in oil, this one has just enough extra virgin olive oil to enrich and enhance the vegetables. A great cook-ahead dish, this is delicious with crusty bread or baked potatoes and salad.

1 large aubergine, about 340g, cut lengthways into 10 slices, each about 3mm thick
2 tablespoons extra virgin olive oil
1 onion, thinly sliced
4 garlic cloves, chopped
½ red pepper, seeded and cut into thin strips
½ green pepper, seeded and cut into thin strips
1 courgette, cut into thin strips
2 tablespoons chopped parsley
6 tomatoes, diced

pinch of sugar
200ml passata
4 tablespoons chopped fresh basil
170g mozzarella cheese, diced
8 black olives, stoned and chopped
salt and pepper
sprigs of fresh basil to garnish

PREPARATION TIME 45 minutes
COOKING TIME 30 minutes
SERVES 4

1 Dice the 2 outer (end) slices of aubergine, with the peel, and set aside to add to the filling. Use 2 teaspoons of the olive oil to brush the remaining 8 aubergine slices sparingly on both sides. Heat a ridged griddle or heavy frying pan and brown the aubergine slices for about 2 minutes on each side or until they are tender but not soft. Set aside on a board. **2** Add the remaining oil to the pan and cook the onion, half of the garlic, the red and green peppers, courgette and reserved diced aubergine for about 5 minutes or until softened. Add the parsley and half of the diced tomatoes, and continue to cook for a further 5–6 minutes. **3** Season the vegetable mixture, add the sugar and pour in the passata. Bring to the boil, then cover and cook over a low heat for about 10 minutes or until the mixture is richly flavoured and thickened. **4** In a bowl, combine the remaining garlic and diced tomatoes with the chopped basil, mozzarella and olives. Set this topping mixture aside. Preheat the oven to 180°C (350°F, gas mark 4). **5** Lightly season the aubergine slices. Place a generous portion of the braised vegetable filling at the wider end of one slice and roll up to enclose the filling. Repeat with the remaining aubergine slices and filling, placing the rolls side by side in an ovenproof dish. **6** Spoon the tomato and mozzarella mixture evenly over the top. Bake for about 30 minutes or until the cheese topping has melted. Garnish with basil sprigs and serve hot or warm.

NUTRIENTS PER SERVING KCAL 245 • CARBOHYDRATE 11g (of which 10g sugars) • PROTEIN 14g • FAT 16g (of which saturated fat 7g) • FIBRE 5g • SODIUM 237mg • SALT 0.6g • VEGETABLE PORTION 4

BAKED AUBERGINE AND APPLE LAYERS

Serve this versatile bake, with its fresh tomato sauce, as a main course or as an accompaniment.

500g aubergines, cut into 1cm slices
Salt and black pepper
300g cooking apples or tart dessert apples,
  cored and cut into 5mm slices

FOR THE SAUCE
2 cloves garlic, crushed
2 tablespoons olive oil
2 tablespoons chopped fresh flat-leaved
  parsley
1 tablespoon chopped fresh thyme

2 tablespoons tomato purée
500g plum tomatoes, peeled, deseeded and
  chopped

TO GARNISH 1 tablespoon chopped fresh herbs,
  such as parsley and thyme

PREPARATION TIME 15 minutes, plus
  30 minutes standing
COOKING TIME 40 minutes
SERVES 4

1 Sprinkle both sides of the aubergine slices with salt, place them in a colander and set aside to drain for 30 minutes. **2** To make the sauce, put all the ingredients in a food processor, or use a hand-held mixer, and blend until smooth. Set aside. **3** Turn the oven on to 220°C (425°F, gas mark 7) and heat a ridged cast-iron griddle or heavy-based frying pan over a medium-high heat. Rinse the aubergine slices and dry them with kitchen paper. Dry-fry them for 2–3 minutes on each side until they have softened and browned. **4** Arrange half the aubergine slices in a single layer in a 25 x 20cm ovenproof dish and cover them with 2 tablespoons of the sauce, spreading it out evenly. Layer all the apple slices on top and cover with another 2 tablespoons of sauce. Top with the remaining aubergines and smooth the remaining sauce over the top. Bake for 30 minutes. **5** Sprinkle the dish with the herbs and serve, hot or at room temperature, with red or brown rice.

NUTRIENTS PER SERVING KCAL 132 • CARBOHYDRATE 17g (of which 14g sugars) • PROTEIN 3g
• FAT 7g (of which saturated fat 1g) • FIBRE 5g • SODIUM 33mg • SALT trace
• VEGETABLE PORTION 2

MEXICAN VEGETABLE AND CORNMEAL PIE

Break through the crisp, golden brown cornmeal topping of this spicy pie to discover a delicious mixture of tastes and textures. Ring the changes with your own favourite ingredients.

1 tablespoon sunflower oil
1 stick celery, chopped
1 large clove garlic, crushed
150g onions, chopped
½ green pepper, chopped
1 teaspoon cayenne pepper
400g canned red kidney beans, drained and rinsed
12 stoned green olives, sliced
1 tablespoon chopped jalapeño peppers
75g canned sweetcorn, drained
400g canned chopped tomatoes
1 tablespoon tomato purée
Salt and black pepper

FOR THE TOPPING
125g cornmeal, or polenta
1 tablespoon plain white flour
2 teaspoons baking powder
1 egg, beaten
100ml skimmed milk
25g half-fat mature Cheddar cheese, grated

PREPARATION TIME 20 minutes, plus 5 minutes standing
COOKING TIME 1 hour
SERVES 4

1 Heat the oven to 200°C (400°F, gas mark 6). Heat the oil in a saucepan over a high heat. Stir in the celery, garlic, onions and green pepper, bring them to a sizzle, then cover, reduce the heat to low and cook for 10 minutes, or until they have softened. Stir in the cayenne pepper and cook for a further 1–2 minutes. **2** Stir in the kidney beans, olives, jalapeño peppers, sweetcorn, canned tomatoes, tomato paste and add salt and pepper to taste. Bring the mixture to the boil and simmer for 5 minutes. Then spoon the mixture into a 3litre ovenproof serving dish. **3** To make the topping, mix together the cornmeal or polenta, flour, ½ teaspoon of salt and the baking powder, then beat in the egg and milk. The mixture should look like a thick batter; if not, add 1–2 tablespoons of milk. **4** Spoon the topping over the vegetables, sprinkle with the cheese and bake for 40 minutes, or until the topping is risen and golden brown. Leave the pie to stand for 5 minutes before serving.

NUTRIENTS PER SERVING KCAL 378 • CARBOHYDRATE 56g (of which 12g sugars) • PROTEIN 19g • FAT 10g (of which saturated fat 3g) • FIBRE 8g • SODIUM 900mg • SALT 2.2g • VEGETABLE PORTION 2

Boiling **broccoli** almost halves its vitamin C content, so it is better to microwave, stir-fry or lightly steam it.

SPICY BROCCOLI AND CAULIFLOWER

Spicy and crisp, this delicious combination of broccoli and cauliflower with capers and pickled green peppercorns is finished off with a tasty double-cheese and breadcrumb topping.

5 cloves garlic
1 green chilli
500g broccoli florets
500g cauliflower florets
2 tablespoons olive oil
Salt and black pepper
50g Emmental cheese

50g Lancashire cheese
3 tablespoons dried breadcrumbs
2 tablespoons capers
1–2 tablespoons pickled green peppercorns

TOTAL TIME 25 minutes
SERVES 4

1 Preheat the grill and put a kettle of water on to boil. **2** Peel and thinly slice the garlic, then rinse, deseed and chop the chilli. Rinse the broccoli and cauliflower florets. **3** Heat the oil in a frying pan or large wok with a lid. Add the garlic and chilli, stir in the broccoli and cauliflower florets, sprinkle with salt and pepper and add 150ml of boiling water. Cover the pan and cook the vegetables over a high heat for 4–5minutes, or until they are tender. Stir or toss them halfway through cooking. **4** Meanwhile, grate the Emmental and Lancashire cheeses and mix them with the breadcrumbs. **5** Stir the capers and peppercorns into the vegetables. Transfer them to a shallow, flameproof dish, sprinkle the cheese and breadcrumb mixture over the top, and place under the grill until the cheese melts and the topping turns golden. Serve hot.

NUTRIENTS PER SERVING KCAL 286 • CARBOHYDRATE 16g (of which 6g sugars) • PROTEIN 20g • FAT 16g (of which saturated fat 6g) • FIBRE 6g • SODIUM 507mg • SALT 1.2g • VEGETABLE PORTION 3

CHUNKY VEGETABLE CRUMBLE

A tasty mixture of root vegetables and creamy butter beans topped with savoury cheese crumble makes a nourishing dish. Sunflower seeds in the crumble add texture and extra protein.

1 tablespoon sunflower oil
1 onion, sliced
2 garlic cloves, crushed
3 carrots, cut into 2cm chunks
2 parsnips, cut into 2cm chunks
250g baby turnips, quartered
350g waxy new potatoes, scrubbed and cut into 2cm chunks
450ml vegetable stock
generous dash of Worcestershire sauce
1 tablespoon tomato purée
2 bay leaves
1 x 410g can butter beans, drained and rinsed

3 tablespoons chopped parsley
salt and pepper

SUNFLOWER SEED CRUMBLE TOPPING
85g wholemeal flour
30g cool butter, diced
75g mature Cheddar cheese, coarsely grated
30g sunflower seeds

PREPARATION TIME 40 minutes
COOKING TIME 20 minutes
SERVES 4

1 Heat the oil in a large saucepan, add the onion and cook gently for 10 minutes or until softened. Add the garlic and cook for 1 more minute. **2** Add the carrots, parsnips, turnips and potatoes. Stir in the stock, Worcestershire sauce, tomato purée and bay leaves. Bring to the boil, then reduce the heat, cover and simmer for 20 minutes, stirring occasionally. **3** Meanwhile, make the crumble topping. Put the flour in a bowl and rub in the butter. Sprinkle over 1½ tablespoons cold water and mix together with a fork to make large crumbs. Stir in the cheese and sunflower seeds. Set aside. **4** Preheat the oven to 190°C (375°F, gas mark 5). Stir the butter beans into the vegetables and cook for a further 5–7 minutes or until the vegetables are just tender. Remove and discard the bay leaves. **5** Remove a large ladleful of the vegetables and stock, and mash until smooth or purée in a blender or processor. Stir the purée into the vegetable mixture in the pan to thicken it slightly. Stir in the parsley, and season with salt and pepper to taste. **6** Spoon the vegetable mixture into a lightly greased 1.7 litre ovenproof dish. Sprinkle the crumble mixture evenly over the top. Bake for 20 minutes or until golden brown.

NUTRIENTS PER SERVING KCAL 465 • CARBOHYDRATE 55g (of which 16g sugars) • PROTEIN 17g • FAT 21g (of which saturated fat 9g) • FIBRE 12.5g • SODIUM 673mg • SALT 1.7g • VEGETABLE PORTION 3

ROASTED VEGETABLE TART

A scattering of fresh herbs and melting cheese add the finishing touches to vegetables baked in a crisp filo crust. Ring the changes with a mixed breadcrumb and grated hard cheese topping.

400g aubergines
400g courgettes
1 red pepper, thickly sliced
1 yellow pepper, thickly sliced
150g red onions, thickly sliced
1 clove garlic, chopped
1 teaspoon chopped fresh rosemary or thyme,
  plus extra fresh sprigs for topping

3 tablespoons olive oil
Salt and black pepper
4 sheets filo pastry, about 125g altogether
75g half-fat mozzarella cheese, shredded

PREPARATION TIME 15 minutes
COOKING TIME 50 minutes-1 hour 10 minutes
SERVES 4

1 Heat the oven to 200°C (400°F, gas mark 6). Cut the aubergines and courgettes into 1cm slices. Arrange all the vegetables in a single layer in a roasting tin, scatter the garlic and rosemary or thyme over them, then drizzle with 2 tablespoons of the olive oil. Season to taste. **2** Roast the vegetables for 40-60 minutes until they have softened and browned. **3** Meanwhile, place a baking sheet in the oven to warm. Line a 20-23cm loose-based tart tin with the sheets of filo pastry, brushing each layer with oil before adding the next. Crumple up any overhanging edges to form a rim. Place the tin on the baking sheet and bake the pastry case for 5–8 minutes until golden brown. **4** Reduce the oven to 160°C (325°F, gas mark 3). Spoon the roasted vegetables into the pastry case and scatter the cheese and chopped rosemary and thyme evenly over the top. Return the tart to the oven for 10 minutes, or until the cheese has just melted. Cut into quarters and serve it warm with a crisp salad and your favourite crusty bread.

NUTRIENTS PER SERVING KCAL 260 • CARBOHYDRATE 28g (of which 10g sugars) • PROTEIN 10g • FAT 12g (of which saturated fat 3g) • FIBRE 4.5g • SODIUM 81mg • SALT trace • VEGETABLE PORTION 3

MEDITERRANEAN CHICKPEA PIE

Enjoy the taste of the Mediterranean with vegetables and chickpeas cooked in red wine, tomatoes and Italian herbs, topped with a cheese, sun-dried tomato and fresh basil mash. Serve with a seasonal green vegetable, such as Savoy cabbage.

2 tablespoons extra virgin olive oil
2 onions, chopped
2 celery sticks, chopped
1 red pepper, seeded and diced
2 garlic cloves, crushed
2 courgettes, sliced
2 cans chickpeas, about 410g each, drained and rinsed
2 cans chopped tomatoes, about 400g each
2 tablespoons sun-dried tomato paste
150ml red wine
2 teaspoons dried Italian herb seasoning
salt and pepper

CHEESE AND TOMATO MASH
1kg potatoes, peeled and cut into chunks
4 tablespoons semi-skimmed milk
1 egg
50g Italian-style premium cheese, freshly grated
50g sun-dried tomatoes in oil, drained and finely chopped
3 tablespoons chopped fresh basil

PREPARATION TIME 55 minutes
COOKING TIME 25 minutes
SERVES 6

1 Heat a tablespoon of the oil in a large pan, add the onions, celery, red pepper and garlic, and sauté for 5 minutes. Add the courgettes, chickpeas, tomatoes with their juice, tomato paste, wine and dried herbs. Season with salt and pepper to taste and mix well. **2** Bring to the boil, then reduce the heat. Cover the pan and simmer for 20 minutes, stirring occasionally. Uncover the pan, increase the heat and cook for a further 10–15 minutes, stirring occasionally, until the liquid has thickened slightly. **3** Meanwhile, cook the potatoes in a saucepan of boiling water for 15–20 minutes or until tender. Preheat the oven to 200°C (400°F, gas mark 6). **4** Drain the potatoes well, then return to the pan. Add the milk and the remaining tablespoon of olive oil, and mash until smooth. Beat in the egg, cheese, sun-dried tomatoes, chopped basil, and salt and pepper to taste. Mix well. **5** Spoon the vegetable mixture into an ovenproof dish. Top with the cheese mash, covering the vegetables completely. Mark the top of the mash decoratively with a fork. **6** Bake the pie for 25 minutes or until the potato topping is nicely browned. Serve hot.

NUTRIENTS PER SERVING KCAL 426 • CARBOHYDRATE 54g (of which 12g sugars) • PROTEIN 18g • FAT 15g (of which saturated fat 3.5g) • FIBRE 8g • SODIUM 404mg • SALT 1g • VEGETABLE PORTION 3

Celery may lower cholesterol and high blood presssure and contains an anti-inflammatory agent that can help to alleviate the painful symptoms of gout.

pa

PASTA AND GRAINS

VEGETABLE PRIMAVERA

The secret of this dish lies in the light cooking of a mixture of fine spring vegetables, which gives them a crisp texture and fresh flavour, and contrasts well with the stuffed pasta.

200g baby carrots
150g baby corn cobs
200g young fine green beans
Salt and black pepper
250g baby or small courgettes
A small handful of fresh parsley or chervil
400g fresh ricotta and spinach tortellini

1 tablespoon olive oil
½ lemon
1 tablespoon wholegrain mustard

TOTAL TIME 30 minutes
SERVES 4

1 Put a large saucepan of water and a kettle on to boil. Preheat the oven to a low setting.
2 Rinse and trim the carrots, corn and beans, and cut them into short lengths if they are large. Plunge the vegetables into the pan of boiling water, add salt, bring back to the boil, then simmer for 4–5 minutes, keeping them slightly crisp. **3** Meanwhile, rinse and trim the courgettes. Cut baby courgettes in half lengthways, small ones into slices, and set aside. Rinse, dry and chop the parsley or chervil. **4** Lift the cooked vegetables from the boiling water with a slotted spoon, put them into a bowl and keep them warm in the oven. Bring the water back to the boil, topping up with more from the kettle if necessary. Add the pasta and boil gently for 5–6 minutes.
5 Meanwhile, heat the olive oil in a large saucepan, add the courgettes and fry them, stirring continuously, for 2–3 minutes. **6** Squeeze the lemon juice into the courgettes, then add the drained vegetables, mustard, and salt and pepper to taste. Toss gently together. **7** Drain the pasta and mix it into the vegetables. Turn onto a warmed serving dish, add a sprinkling of parsley or chervil, and serve hot.

NUTRIENTS PER SERVING KCAL 537 • CARBOHYDRATE 53g (of which 11g sugars) • PROTEIN 26g • FAT 25g (of which saturated fat 13g) • FIBRE 7g • SODIUM 615mg • SALT 1.5g • VEGETABLE PORTION 2

RADIATORI WITH FLAGEOLET BEANS IN TOMATO DRESSING

Beans and pasta eaten together provide an excellent source of protein. Here, tender flageolet beans partner chunky pasta shapes in a salad with celery, red pepper and canned artichoke hearts. A well-flavoured dressing marries the ingredients perfectly.

225g radiatori (pasta grills) or other shapes
1 can artichoke hearts, about 400g, drained and quartered
4 ripe tomatoes, skinned and cut into thin wedges
3 celery sticks, thinly sliced
1 red pepper, seeded and cut into thin strips
1 can flageolet beans, about 400g, drained and rinsed
2 tablespoons finely shredded fresh basil

TOMATO DRESSING
2 tablespoons sun-dried tomato paste
1 garlic clove, crushed
2 tablespoons extra virgin olive oil
2 tablespoons lemon juice
1 teaspoon caster sugar
salt and pepper

PREPARATION TIME 25–35 minutes, plus cooling
SERVES 4

1 Cook the pasta in boiling water for 10–12 minutes, or according to the packet instructions, until al dente. Drain the pasta thoroughly and turn it into a large bowl. **2** Add the artichoke hearts, tomatoes, celery, red pepper, flageolet beans and basil. Gently toss the pasta and vegetables together. The cold vegetables will cool the pasta, keeping the pieces firm and separate, while the warmth of the pasta will bring out the flavours of the vegetables. **3** Whisk all the ingredients for the dressing together until thoroughly blended. Add seasoning to taste and pour the dressing over the salad. Lightly toss the salad to coat all the ingredients with dressing, then set aside until cool. Transfer the salad to individual bowls or one large dish to serve.

NUTRIENTS PER SERVING KCAL 400 • CARBOHYDRATE 68g (of which 10g sugars)
• PROTEIN 18.5g • FAT 7.5g (of which saturated fat 1.5g) • FIBRE 9g • SODIUM 438mg
• SALT 1.5g • VEGETABLE PORTION 2

STUFFED GIANT PASTA SHELLS

A creamy sauce of courgettes, low-fat ricotta and walnuts reinterprets an Italian classic, and makes a sophisticated dressing for pasta shells filled with a spinach and herb stuffing.

500g spinach, trimmed
3 courgettes, thinly sliced
4 garlic cloves, chopped
500ml vegetable stock
250g ricotta cheese
100g walnuts, coarsely chopped
85g Italian-style premium cheese, freshly grated
3 tablespoons chopped fresh chervil or marjoram
3 tablespoons chopped fresh chives or 3 small shallots, finely chopped
3 tablespoons chopped fresh basil

1 egg, lightly beaten
12 no-precook conchiglie grande (giant pasta shells for stuffing)
55g Edam cheese, grated
2 tablespoons finely shredded fresh basil or tiny basil leaves
salt and pepper

PREPARATION TIME 40 minutes, plus 5 minutes standing
COOKING TIME 30 minutes
SERVES 4

1 Wash the spinach well and place the wet leaves in a large saucepan. Cover and cook over a high heat for about 3 minutes, shaking the pan frequently. When the spinach is just tender and wilted, tip it into a colander and leave it to drain and cool. **2** Meanwhile, place the courgettes and half the garlic in a saucepan. Pour in the stock and bring to the boil. Cook over a high heat for about 3 minutes or until the courgettes are just tender. **3** Purée the courgettes and stock in a blender or food processor until smooth, adding half the ricotta cheese, the walnuts, 2 tablespoons of the Italian-style cheese and seasoning to taste. The resulting sauce should have a consistency halfway between single and double cream, slightly more runny than a coating sauce should be. **4** When the spinach is cool enough to handle, squeeze it dry in small handfuls and chop it coarsely. Mix the spinach with the chervil or marjoram, chives or shallots, basil, the remaining garlic and ricotta cheese, the egg and seasoning to taste. **5** Preheat the oven to 190°C (375°F, gas mark 5). Use a small teaspoon to stuff the pasta shells with the spinach mixture, and arrange them in an ovenproof dish. **6** Pour the sauce over the stuffed shells and sprinkle with the remaining grated Italian-style cheese. Cover the dish tightly with foil and bake for 30 minutes. **7** Sprinkle the Edam cheese and basil over the cooked stuffed pasta and leave to stand for 5 minutes, uncovered, until the cheese melts, then serve.

NUTRIENTS PER SERVING KCAL 630 • CARBOHYDRATE 39g (of which 6g sugars) • PROTEIN 34g • FAT 38g (of which saturated fat 13g) • FIBRE 5.5g • SODIUM 865mg • SALT 2g • VEGETABLE PORTION 1

BAKED RIGATONI WITH AUBERGINE

Aubergine adds flavour and texture to a hearty vegetarian pasta dish topped with a crisp layer of breadcrumbs and cheese. The rich tomato sauce could be made in advance, then the dish quickly assembled and baked as required. Serve with a green side salad.

2 tablespoons extra virgin olive oil
1 large onion, chopped
2 garlic cloves, crushed
4 tablespoons red wine
2 cans chopped tomatoes in rich tomato juice, about 400g each
5 sun-dried tomatoes packed in oil, about 45g in total, drained and chopped
1 aubergine, cut into 1cm cubes
2 tablespoons chopped fresh oregano

225g rigatoni or other chunky pasta tube shapes, such as penne
30g fresh Granary breadcrumbs
30g Italian-style premium cheese, freshly grated
salt and pepper

PREPARATION TIME 35 minutes
COOKING TIME 15–20 minutes
SERVES 4

1 Heat the oil in a large saucepan, add the onion and cook gently for 4–5 minutes, stirring frequently, until it has softened and turned lightly golden. Add the garlic and cook gently for a further 1–2 minutes. **2** Pour in the wine and allow it to bubble for a few minutes, then add the canned tomatoes with their juice, the sun-dried tomatoes, aubergine and oregano. Bring to the boil, then reduce the heat, cover and simmer gently for 15–20 minutes, stirring occasionally.
3 Meanwhile, cook the pasta in a large pan of boiling water for 10–12 minutes, or according to the packet instructions, until al dente. Drain well. **4** Set the oven to 200°C (400°F, gas mark 6). Season the tomato sauce with salt and pepper to taste. Tip the cooked pasta into a large, lightly greased ovenproof dish. Pour over the sauce and mix well together so that all the pasta is coated.
5 Combine the breadcrumbs and cheese in a bowl, and sprinkle this mixture evenly over the top of the pasta. Bake for 15–20 minutes or until the sauce is bubbling and the top is golden brown and crisp. Serve hot.

NUTRIENTS PER SERVING KCAL 425 • **CARBOHYDRATE 59g (of which 12g sugars)** • **PROTEIN 14g** • **FAT 15g (of which saturated fat 3g)** • **FIBRE 6g** • **SODIUM 200mg** • **SALT 0.5g** • **VEGETABLE PORTION 2**

KASHTOURI

This Egyptian dish of rice, macaroni and lentils in a spicy tomato sauce makes a quick light meal.

150g risotto rice, such as arborio
Salt and black pepper
150g short-cut macaroni
2 teaspoons olive oil
150g onions, chopped
2 large cloves garlic, crushed
1 teaspoon cayenne pepper or paprika
1 teaspoon ground coriander

400g canned chopped tomatoes
400g canned green lentils, including liquid
2 tablespoons chopped fresh parsley

PREPARATION TIME 5 minutes
COOKING TIME 20 minutes
SERVES 4

1 Bring a large saucepan of water to the boil, add the rice and a pinch of salt, return the water to the boil, then reduce the heat and simmer for 5 minutes. Add the macaroni and stir, increase the heat to medium and cook for a further 10 minutes, or until both rice and macaroni are tender. Drain and set aside in a colander. **2** Meanwhile, put the oil and 2 tablespoons of water in a saucepan, add the onions and garlic and sauté for 5 minutes or until they have softened. Stir in the spices and cook for a further 1 minute. **3** Add the tomatoes and lentils and their canned liquid to the onions, season to taste and bring the mixture to the boil. Reduce the heat and simmer for 10 minutes, stirring occasionally. **4** Mix in the rice and macaroni then add the parsley, reserving a small amount for garnish, and heat through. Serve hot, garnished with parsley.

NUTRIENTS PER SERVING KCAL 450 • CARBOHYDRATE 81g (of which 6g sugars) • PROTEIN 17g • FAT 7g (of which saturated fat 1g) • FIBRE 6g • SODIUM 47mg • SALT 0.1g • VEGETABLE PORTION 1

CATALAN-STYLE PASTA IN TOMATO BROTH

Make pasta Spanish style – in a thick fresh sauce enlivened by the flavour of herbs. Make as a side dish or as a light meal in its own right.

500g tomatoes, chopped
1 whole head garlic, separated into individual
   cloves and peeled
150g onions, chopped
A strip of orange zest, about 5cm long
2 bay leaves and 2 sprigs of fresh thyme, tied
   together
10–12 strands saffron
600 ml vegetable stock
A pinch of caster sugar
1 tablespoon olive oil
225g vermicelli, broken into pieces
Salt and black pepper

TO GARNISH sprigs of fresh basil

PREPARATION TIME 20 minutes
COOKING TIME 30 minutes
SERVES 4

1 Put the tomatoes, garlic, onions, orange zest, herbs, saffron, stock and sugar into a saucepan and bring to the boil. Cover, reduce the heat and simmer for 20 minutes. **2** Discard the herbs and zest, then purée the broth in a food processor or with a hand-held mixer. **3** Return the purée to the pan and stir in the oil, vermicelli and some salt and pepper to taste. Bring to the boil then simmer, uncovered, for 8–10 minutes, stirring occasionally, until the pasta is cooked and the broth has thickened. Season to taste and serve, garnished with fresh basil.

NUTRIENTS PER SERVING KCAL 280 • CARBOHYDRATE 55g (of which 8g sugars) • PROTEIN 7g
• FAT 4g (of which saturated fat 1g) • FIBRE 3.5g • SODIUM 313mg • SALT 0.8g
• VEGETABLE PORTION 2

FETTUCCINE WITH BROCCOLI

A buttery Dijon mustard sauce with basil and parsley, makes an unusual spicy dressing for ribbon noodles of fresh egg pasta, crunchy green florets of fresh broccoli and bright cherry tomatoes.

10 fresh basil leaves
3 sprigs of parsley
2 spring onions
2 small cloves garlic
2 tablespoons Dijon mustard
125g softened butter
2 large heads broccoli, to give 550g florets
1 tablespoon olive oil
Salt and black pepper
500g fresh fettuccine, or tagliatelle

TO GARNISH 10 cherry tomatoes

TIME 20 minutes
SERVES 4

1 Put a large saucepan of water on to boil for the pasta. Rinse and dry the basil and parsley and chop them finely. Trim and rinse the spring onions; finely slice the green tops and set them aside, then slice the rest. Peel and crush the garlic. **2** Blend the mustard and butter in a bowl then stir in the herbs, white spring onion and garlic, crushing them against the bottom of the bowl to release their flavours. Set aside. **3** Rinse and trim the broccoli into florets. Add the oil, salt, pasta and broccoli to the boiling water, return to the boil and cook for 4 minutes, or until the pasta is al dente. **4** Meanwhile, rinse and halve the cherry tomatoes. **5** Thoroughly drain the pasta and broccoli. Quickly melt the flavoured butter in the pasta pan. Return the pasta and broccoli to the pan and toss them gently in the butter over a moderate heat until the pasta is well coated, but do not allow it to fry. **6** Transfer the pasta onto a serving platter, season, and garnish with the green onion tops and tomatoes.

NUTRIENTS PER SERVING KCAL 651 • CARBOHYDRATE 73g (of which 5g sugars) • PROTEIN 20g • FAT 32g (of which saturated fat 17g) • FIBRE 4g • SODIUM 239mg • SALT 0.6g • VEGETABLE PORTION 2

TAGLIATELLE WITH SUMMER VEGETABLES

Choose vegetables at the peak of freshness for this light pasta dish, which uses lemon, tarragon and garlic to bring out their delicate flavours. It's perfect for a light lunch or supper on a hot day.

250g thin asparagus
150g green beans
200g small courgettes
150g young leeks
Salt and black pepper
500g fresh egg tagliatelle, or other thin pasta
1 tablespoon olive oil
1 clove garlic, finely chopped

4 tablespoons lemon juice, or to taste
2 teaspoons chopped fresh tarragon
2–3 tablespoons finely chopped fresh
  flat-leaved parsley

PREPARATION TIME 15 minutes
COOKING TIME 15–20 minutes
SERVES 4

1 Put two saucepans of water on to boil. Trim off the woody stems of the asparagus and cut the spears into 2.5cm lengths. Trim the green beans and cut them in half. Slice the courgettes thinly. Trim and cut the leeks into quarters lengthways, then into 1cm slices. **2** Put the asparagus and beans into one pan of boiling water and cook them for 4 minutes, or until just tender. Drain, refresh them with cold water and set aside. **3** Add the pasta to the remaining pan of boiling water and cook according to the instructions on the packet. **4** Meanwhile, heat the olive oil in a wok or heavy-based nonstick frying pan over a medium-high heat. Add the garlic and stir-fry for 30 seconds, then add the courgettes and leeks and stir-fry for 3 minutes, or until the courgettes are tender but not too soft. **5** Add the asparagus and beans to the wok or pan and stir-fry for 1 minute, then mix in the lemon juice and tarragon. Remove from the heat and season with salt and pepper to taste. **6** Drain the pasta, reserving the cooking water. Stir the pasta into the vegetables, using a few teaspoons of the cooking water to moisten, if necessary. Sprinkle with the parsley and extra black pepper and serve.

NUTRIENTS PER SERVING KCAL 400 • **CARBOHYDRATE 73g (of which 6g sugars)** • **PROTEIN 18g**
• **FAT 7g (of which saturated fat 0.5g)** • **FIBRE 3g** • **SODIUM 37mg** • **SALT trace**
• **VEGETABLE PORTION 2**

Pasta is an excellent source of slow-release carbohydrates for sustained energy.

FLAGEOLET BEAN AND LENTIL LASAGNE

This colourful main dish is built up with layers of red pepper, lentil and bean sauce, sheets of lasagne and sliced artichoke hearts. The creamy topping is a combination of cheeses.

200g no-precook lasagne sheets, about 12
1 can artichoke hearts in water, about 400g, drained, rinsed and sliced
150g ricotta cheese
100ml semi-skimmed milk
3 tablespoons freshly grated Italian-style premium cheese

LENTIL AND BEAN SAUCE
1 tablespoon sunflower oil
1 large red onion, thinly sliced
100g split red lentils
2 large red peppers, seeded and diced
1 large carrot, thinly sliced
2 celery sticks, thinly sliced
550ml vegetable stock
1 bay leaf
2 cans flageolet beans, about 410g each, drained and rinsed
salt and pepper

PREPARATION TIME 45 minutes, plus 5 minutes standing
COOKING TIME 40 minutes
SERVES 6

1 To make the sauce, heat the oil in a saucepan, add the onion and cook gently for 10 minutes or until softened. Add the lentils, red peppers, carrot, celery, stock and bay leaf. Bring to the boil, then reduce the heat and simmer for about 25 minutes or until the lentils and vegetables are very tender. **2** Remove the bay leaf, then purée in a blender or food processor, or using a hand-held blender directly in the pan, until smooth. Season with salt and pepper to taste, and stir in the flageolet beans. **3** Preheat the oven to 190°C (375°F, gas mark 5). Spoon about one-quarter of the sauce over the bottom of a large, greased ovenproof dish. Cover with one-third of the lasagne sheets, then top with half of the remaining sauce. Arrange half the sliced artichoke hearts over the sauce. Repeat with another layer of pasta, then the rest of the sauce and the rest of the artichokes. Finish with the last of the pasta sheets. **4** Put the ricotta cheese into a bowl and stir in the milk until smooth. Season with pepper to taste. Spoon the ricotta sauce over the lasagne, then scatter the grated cheese on top. **5** Bake for 40 minutes or until bubbling and the top is golden. Remove from the oven and leave to stand for 5 minutes before serving.

NUTRIENTS PER SERVING KCAL 400 • CARBOHYDRATE 65g (of which 15g sugars) • PROTEIN 21g • FAT 8g (of which saturated fat 3g) • FIBRE 11g • SODIUM 829mg • SALT 2g • VEGETABLE PORTION 2

GRILLED VEGETABLE COUSCOUS WITH CHILLED TOMATO SAUCE

Lightly charred vegetables and herbs lend a brilliant flavour to this easy-to-make couscous dish.

250g couscous
3 red peppers
200g leeks
200g courgettes
150g fennel
1 tablespoon olive oil
Juice of 2 lemons
8 fresh mint leaves, shredded
2 tablespoons chopped fresh parsley
Salt and black pepper

FOR THE SAUCE
2 tablespoons sherry vinegar or white wine
 vinegar
4 teaspoons caster sugar
700ml tomato passata
450g plum tomatoes
2 tablespoons chopped fresh basil

TO GARNISH 200g Greek yoghurt;
fresh basil leaves

PREPARATION TIME 30 minutes
COOKING TIME 20 minutes
SERVES 6

1 Heat the grill to its highest setting. Put the couscous into a large heatproof bowl and pour 400ml of boiling water over it. Stir and leave to stand for 20 minutes. **2** Meanwhile, make the sauce. Heat the vinegar and sugar in a small saucepan, stirring until the sugar has dissolved, then allow this syrup to cool a little. **3** Put the passata into a large bowl. Dice the tomatoes and add them to the bowl with the basil and the vinegar syrup. Season with salt and plenty of black pepper, then chill until required. **4** Cut the peppers in half lengthways and grill them, cut side down, until the skin is well blackened. Transfer them to a bowl, cover it with cling film and leave it to cool for 2–3 minutes. **5** Thickly slice the leeks and courgettes and cut the fennel into thin wedges, chopping and reserving any leaves. Spread out the leeks, courgettes and fennel wedges on the grill pan, brush them all over with oil and grill for 5–10 minutes until lightly browned, turning them over halfway through cooking and removing each piece as soon as it is done. **6** When the peppers are cool enough to handle, skin and deseed them, then dice the flesh and add it to the couscous, with the other grilled vegetables. Stir in the lemon juice, mint, parsley and fennel leaves, and season to taste. **7** Serve the couscous at room temperature. Pile it in mounds on individual dishes, surround with a moat of chilled tomato sauce, spoon a little yoghurt onto the sauce and garnish with basil leaves.

NUTRIENTS PER SERVING KCAL 234 • CARBOHYDRATE 40g (of which 19g sugars) • PROTEIN 7g
• FAT 6g (of which saturated fat 2g) • FIBRE 4.5g • SODIUM 152mg • SALT 0.38g
• VEGETABLE PORTION 2

VEGETABLE COUSCOUS

Sweet winter vegetables and pulses, mingled with dried apricots and hot spices for a Middle Eastern flavour, make a warm and comforting stew to serve with couscous.

1 small onion
15g butter
1 tablespoon olive oil
2 small carrots
½ small swede
1 medium parsnip
A pinch of cayenne pepper
A pinch of turmeric
½ teaspoon ground ginger
½ teaspoon ground cinnamon
A pinch of saffron threads, optional
Salt and black pepper
50g ready-to-eat dried apricots
60g frozen petit pois
100g canned chickpeas
125g couscous

TO GARNISH 2 sprigs of fresh coriander

TOTAL TIME 30 minutes
SERVES 2

1 Put a kettle of water on to boil. Peel and chop the onion. Heat the butter and olive oil in a large, heavy, flameproof casserole. Add the onion and fry gently until soft. **2** Meanwhile, peel the carrots, swede and parsnip. Cut them into 1cm chunks and add them to the onions as you go. Stir in the cayenne pepper, turmeric, ginger, cinnamon and the saffron threads, if using, and season to taste with salt and black pepper. **3** Chop the apricots and add them, with the petit pois. Drain, rinse and add the chickpeas. Add 300ml of boiling water and bring it back to the boil. Reduce the heat, cover and simmer for 15 minutes. **4** Meanwhile, pour 225ml of boiling water into a saucepan, add the couscous and stir it, then turn off the heat and leave it to stand, covered, until the vegetables are ready. Meanwhile, rinse and dry the coriander and set it aside. **5** Check the couscous and season to taste. Break it up with a fork and transfer it to a serving dish. **6** Taste and adjust the seasoning of the vegetables, then spoon them and their broth over the couscous. Garnish the dish with a sprig of coriander and serve.

NUTRIENTS PER SERVING KCAL 480 • CARBOHYDRATE 75g (of which 28g sugars) • PROTEIN 13g • FAT 15g (of which saturated fat 5g) • FIBRE 12g • SODIUM 170mg • SALT 0.4g • VEGETABLE PORTION 2

SUMMER TABBOULEH

Bulghur wheat is perfect with crisp, just-cooked summer vegetables mixed with handfuls of fresh herbs and tossed with a lively honey and mustard dressing to give it an extra bite.

250g bulghur (cracked) wheat
200g fine green beans
200g frozen peas
Salt
5 large spring onions
300g tomatoes
1 lemon
A large handful of fresh parsley
A large handful of fresh mint
A large handful of chives or dill

TO SERVE 2 Little Gem lettuces

FOR THE DRESSING
3 tablespoons extra virgin olive oil
1 tablespoon red wine vinegar
1 teaspoon honey
1 tablespoon Dijon mustard
Salt and black pepper

TOTAL TIME 30 minutes
SERVES 4

1 Put a kettle of water on to boil. Put the bulgur wheat in a saucepan with 700ml of cold water. Bring to the boil, reduce the heat and simmer for 8–10 minutes, until the bulgur wheat has absorbed all the water. **2** Meanwhile, rinse, top and tail the green beans and chop them into 2.5cm pieces. Put them into a saucepan with the frozen peas. Cover with boiling water, add a little salt, return to the boil, cook for 1–2 minutes, then drain. **3** Rinse, dry, trim and thinly slice the spring onions. Rinse, dry and dice the tomatoes. Wash any wax from the lemon, grate the rind and squeeze the juice. Add them all to the bulgur wheat and fluff up the mixture with a fork. **4** Add the beans and peas to the tabbouleh. Rinse, dry and chop the herbs and add them. Rinse and dry the lettuce leaves and set aside. **5** To make the honey and mustard dressing, whisk all the ingredients together in a bowl, then pour it over the tabbouleh and mix well, then serve with lettuce leaves.

NUTRIENTS PER SERVING KCAL 382 • CARBOHYDRATE 60g (of which 8g sugars) • PROTEIN 12g • FAT 11g (of which saturated fat 1.5g) • FIBRE 4.5g • SODIUM 13mg • SALT 0.3g • VEGETABLE PORTION 2

BULGHUR WHEAT PILAF WITH NUTS AND SEEDS

Although high in fat, nuts and seeds are extremely nutritious, and just a handful gives a pleasing crunch. Bulghur wheat makes a satisfying base for this pilaf and adds fibre and B vitamins.

150g onions, thinly sliced
800ml vegetable stock
300g bulghur wheat
25g unsalted, raw cashew nuts
25g pumpkin seeds
1 tablespoon sesame seeds
1 pomegranate, or 1 dessert apple,
  or 6 apricots

2 tablespoons chopped fresh mint
Salt and black pepper

TO GARNISH sprigs of fresh mint

PREPARATION TIME 10 minutes
COOKING TIME 20 minutes
SERVES 4

1 Sauté the onions in 2 tablespoons of the stock over a medium-high heat for 2–3 minutes, stirring occasionally, until the onions have softened and the liquid evaporated. Heat the grill to high. **2** Stir the bulghur wheat and the remaining stock into the pan and bring to the boil. Then cover and simmer gently over a low heat, stirring occasionally, for 12–15 minutes until the bulghur is tender and the liquid has been absorbed. **3** Meanwhile, toast the cashew nuts under the grill for 30 seconds, or until they are golden. Place the pumpkin and sesame seeds in a small frying pan and dry-fry them for 3–5 seconds over a high heat shaking the pan until the seeds begin to pop. Stir all the nuts and seeds into the bulghur wheat. **4** Cut the pomegranate into quarters and scoop the seeds and juice into the bulghur wheat. If pomegranates are not available, add chopped apple or apricots instead. Stir in the mint and adjust the seasoning to taste. Serve hot or at room temperature, garnished with sprigs of mint.

NUTRIENTS PER SERVING KCAL 390 • CARBOHYDRATE 67g (of which 9g sugars) • PROTEIN 12g • FAT 10g (of which saturated fat 1g) • FIBRE 2.5g • SODIUM 294mg • SALT 0.7g • VEGETABLE PORTION 0

POLENTA WITH A RICH MUSHROOM SAUCE

Satisfying Italian cornmeal is topped with a dark sauce combining dried and fresh mushrooms in this luxurious main course dish. Serve it on its own, or as an accompaniment to other foods.

300g instant polenta
2 teaspoons salt

FOR THE MUSHROOM SAUCE
20g dried wild mushrooms
2 tablespoons olive oil
4 cloves garlic, roughly chopped
1kg button or chestnut mushrooms, or a mixture of the two, thickly sliced
1 tablespoon tomato purée
2 teaspoons dried thyme

50ml red wine
5 teaspoons brandy
Salt and black pepper

TO GARNISH chopped fresh parsley and sprigs of thyme

PREPARATION TIME 10 minutes, plus 30 minutes soaking
COOKING TIME 30 minutes
SERVES 4

1 Put a kettle on to boil. Put the dried mushrooms into a heatproof bowl, cover with boiling water and leave them to soak for 30 minutes. **2** Meanwhile, heat the olive oil in a large saucepan over a medium-high heat. Add the garlic and stir-fry for 15 seconds, then add the fresh mushrooms and continue stir-frying for 10 minutes, or until they have wilted. **3** Strain the soaking liquid off the wild mushrooms through a fine sieve lined with muslin or kitchen paper, and add 50ml of it to the cooked mushrooms. **4** Roughly chop the rehydrated wild mushrooms and add them to the pan with the tomato purée, thyme, wine and brandy. Season to taste and simmer, covered, for 20 minutes, or until you have a thin, richly flavoured sauce. **5** Meanwhile, put the polenta and salt into a large saucepan and pour in 1.4 litres of water, whisking continuously to prevent any lumps. Bring the mixture to the boil, then simmer for 10 minutes, stirring frequently until it becomes firm but not stiff. **6** Arrange spoonfuls of the polenta on individual plates, spoon the mushroom sauce alongside and garnish with the parsley and thyme.

NUTRIENTS PER SERVING KCAL 377 • CARBOHYDRATE 58g (of which 1g sugars) • PROTEIN 12g • FAT 8g (of which saturated fat 1g) • FIBRE 2g • SODIUM 1006mg • SALT 2.5g • VEGETABLE PORTION 1

SQUASH AND TALEGGIO RISOTTO

This tasty risotto makes an excellent family meal. The combination of rice and fresh vegetables, gently cooked with white wine, stock and rosemary, then with creamy Italian taleggio cheese stirred in at the end, creates a nutritious dish packed with flavour.

2 tablespoons extra virgin olive oil
6 shallots, chopped
2 garlic cloves, crushed
500g butternut squash, peeled, seeded and diced
450ml vegetable stock
225g risotto rice
225g chestnut mushrooms, sliced
250ml dry white wine
1 tablespoon chopped fresh rosemary
225g taleggio cheese, rinded and diced
salt and pepper
sprigs of fresh rosemary to garnish

PREPARATION TIME 20 minutes
COOKING TIME 35 minutes
SERVES 4

1 Heat the oil in a large saucepan, add the shallots and garlic, and cook for 2 minutes or until the shallots begin to soften. Add the squash and cook for a further 10 minutes, stirring occasionally. **2** Meanwhile, put the vegetable stock into a saucepan and bring just to simmering point. Reduce the heat so the stock stays hot. **3** Add the rice to the squash and cook for 1 minute, stirring. Stir in the mushrooms, then add the wine and chopped rosemary. Bring it just to the boil and bubble gently until most of the wine has been absorbed, stirring frequently. **4** Add a ladleful of the hot stock and simmer until it has been absorbed, stirring frequently. Continue adding the stock gradually, in this way, waiting for each addition to be absorbed before adding more. When all the stock has been added, the rice should be tender but still firm and the risotto should have a creamy texture. Season with salt and pepper to taste. **5** Remove the risotto from the heat. Add the cheese and stir in gently until it starts to melt. Garnish it with fresh rosemary sprigs and serve it immediately, with a green, leafy salad to make a complete meal.

NUTRIENTS PER SERVING KCAL 513 • CARBOHYDRATE 50g (of which 5g sugars) • PROTEIN 18g • FAT 22g (of which saturated fat 10g) • FIBRE 2g • SODIUM 506mg • SALT 1.2g • VEGETABLE PORTION 2

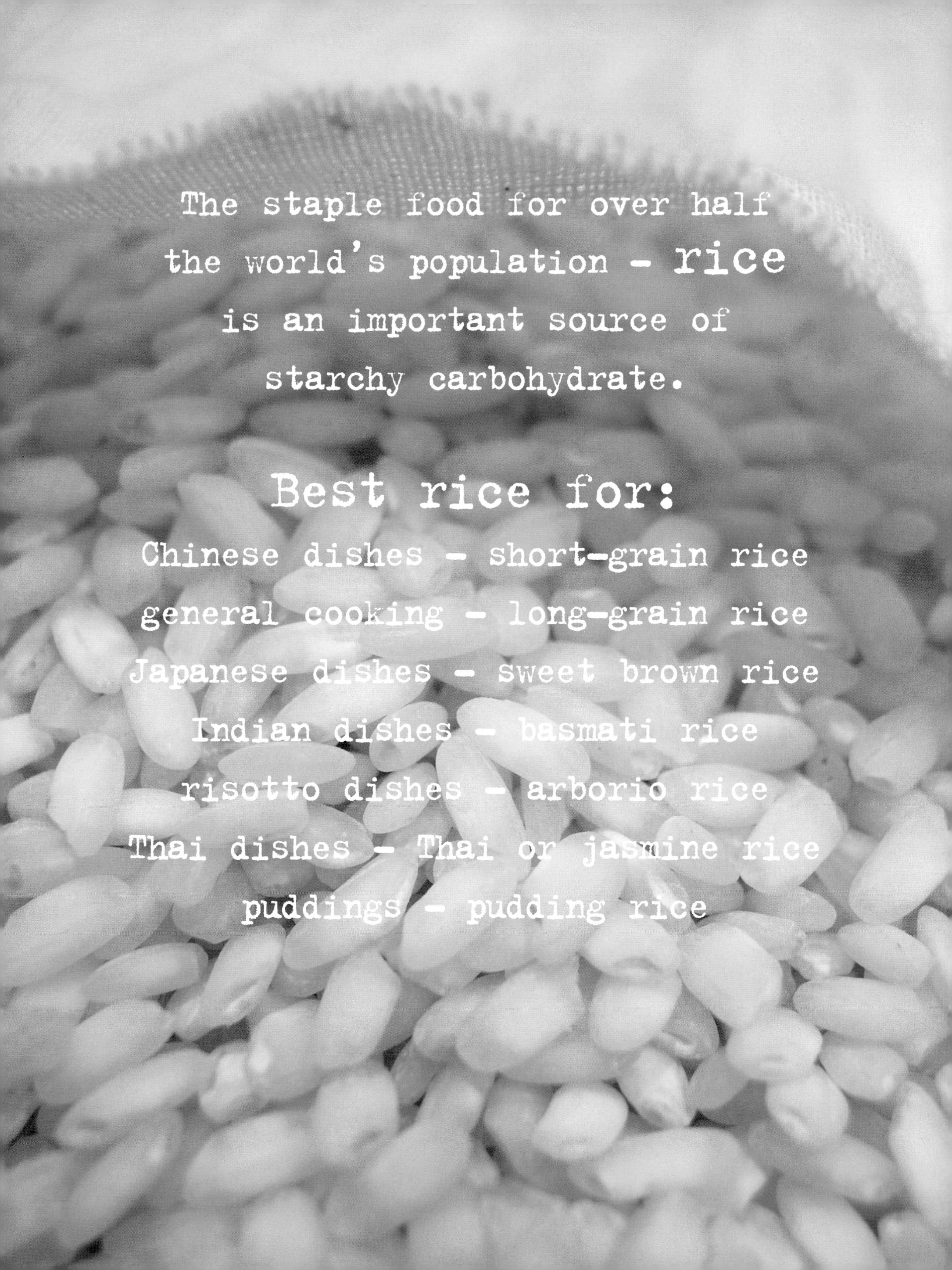

The staple food for over half
the world's population – rice
is an important source of
starchy carbohydrate.

Best rice for:

Chinese dishes – short-grain rice

general cooking – long-grain rice

Japanese dishes – sweet brown rice

Indian dishes – basmati rice

risotto dishes – arborio rice

Thai dishes – Thai or jasmine rice

puddings – pudding rice

TOMATO RISOTTO

A simple risotto of fresh and sun-dried tomatoes is an easy dish for a light lunch or supper.

1 tablespoon olive oil
60g onions or shallots, finely chopped
1 clove garlic, crushed
500ml tomato juice
200g risotto rice, such as arborio
1 tablespoon tomato purée
100g plum tomatoes, peeled, deseeded and diced
50g sun-dried tomatoes, drained, dried and cut into strips

2 tablespoons fresh torn basil leaves
Salt and black pepper

TO GARNISH a few fresh basil leaves
TO SERVE 50g Italian-style premium cheese, grated

PREPARATION TIME 10 minutes
COOKING TIME 30 minutes
SERVES 4

1 Heat the oil in a large nonstick saucepan. Add the onions or shallots and garlic and sauté gently for 10 minutes, or until they are softened but not coloured. **2** Put the tomato juice in another pan and bring it to simmering point. **3** Add the rice to the onions and cook for a further 1–2 minutes, stirring frequently, until the rice becomes transparent. **4** Add a small ladleful of tomato juice to the rice mixture and stir continuously until all the juice has been absorbed. Repeat, stirring after each ladleful of juice has been added, and cook for 10–15 minutes until the rice is tender and has a creamy consistency, adding more water if necessary. **5** Stir the tomato purée, fresh and sun-dried tomatoes and basil leaves into the rice and season to taste. **6** Serve garnished with basil and pass round the grated cheese separately.

NUTRIENTS PER SERVING KCAL 288 • CARBOHYDRATE 46g (of which 6g sugars) • PROTEIN 10g • FAT 8g (of which saturated fat 3g) • FIBRE 1.5g • SODIUM 396mg • SALT 1g • VEGETABLE PORTION 1

EMERALD RISOTTO

Young leaves of baby spinach have a vivid colour and an extra-fresh flavour that is packed with goodness. Try this risotto for a healthy supper that requires little from the cook except stirring.

1.2 litres vegetable stock, or 4 tablespoons vegetable bouillon powder
5 tablespoons white wine
250g baby spinach
4 tablespoons virgin olive oil
1 small onion
2 cloves garlic

350g risotto rice (arborio, carnaroli or vialone)
Salt and black pepper
Whole nutmeg for grating

TOTAL TIME 30 minutes
SERVES 4

1 Bring the stock to the boil in a saucepan, or stir the bouillon powder into 1.2 litres of boiling water. Add the wine, reduce the heat and leave to simmer. **2** Rinse the spinach leaves, chop them roughly and set them aside. **3** Heat the oil in a large saucepan or wok. Peel and finely chop the onion and garlic and fry them gently for 2–3 minutes until soft but not brown. Then add the rice and stir-fry until the grains are translucent and coated with oil. **4** Add a ladleful of stock, adjust the heat to maintain a gentle boil and stir until most of the liquid has been absorbed. Keep adding stock, a ladleful at a time, and stir constantly for about 15 minutes, until the rice is almost cooked. **5** Add the spinach and more stock and boil and stir until the rice is cooked – risotto rice should retain a bite, but the mixture should be of a soft, dropping consistency. **6** Season to taste with salt, pepper and some freshly grated nutmeg. Serve straight from the pan.

NUTRIENTS PER SERVING KCAL 448 • CARBOHYDRATE 73g (of which 2g sugars) • PROTEIN 8g • FAT 14g (of which saturated fat 2g) • FIBRE 2g • SODIUM 680mg • SALT 1.7g • VEGETABLE PORTION 1

CURRIED LENTIL AND VEGETABLE PILAF

Curries usually take a long time to prepare and cook, but by using ready-prepared vegetables and ginger and garlic bottled in oil, this one-dish meal, rich in protein and other essential nutrients, can be on the table in half an hour.

100g creamed coconut
900ml vegetable stock or water
2 tablespoons sunflower oil
1½ teaspoons cumin seeds
2 teaspoons ground coriander
1 teaspoon bottled chopped root ginger in oil, drained
1 teaspoon bottled chopped garlic in oil, drained
½ teaspoon cayenne pepper, or to taste
200g basmati rice, rinsed
200g red lentils

500g prepared mixed vegetables, such as carrots, beans, broccoli and cauliflower
salt and pepper
chopped fresh coriander or parsley to garnish

TO SERVE 2 bananas, finely grated zest of 1 lime, lime juice to taste

PREPARATION AND COOKING TIME about 30 minutes
SERVES 4

1 Grate the creamed coconut into a saucepan and add the stock. Bring to a simmer over a moderate heat, stirring occasionally until the coconut has melted. **2** Meanwhile, heat the oil in a large flameproof casserole or frying pan with a lid. Add the cumin seeds and stir-fry over a moderately high heat until they begin to sizzle and give off their aroma. Stir in the ground coriander, ginger, garlic and cayenne pepper and stir-fry for about 1 minute. **3** Stir in the rice, lentils and vegetables. Pour in the coconut stock and stir to mix everything together. Bring to the boil, then reduce the heat to low, cover and simmer for 20 minutes, without removing the lid, until the rice and lentils are tender and all the liquid has been absorbed. **4** Just before the pilaf finishes cooking, slice the bananas into a bowl. Add the lime zest and sprinkle over lime juice to taste. **5** When the pilaf is ready, adjust the seasoning if necessary, and fluff up the rice with a fork. Sprinkle with the chopped coriander or parsley and serve at once, with the bananas.

NUTRIENTS PER SERVING KCAL 560 • CARBOHYDRATE 87g (of which 18g sugars) • PROTEIN 20g • FAT 16g (of which saturated fat 9g) • FIBRE 5g • SODIUM 627mg • SALT 1.5g • VEGETABLE PORTION 2

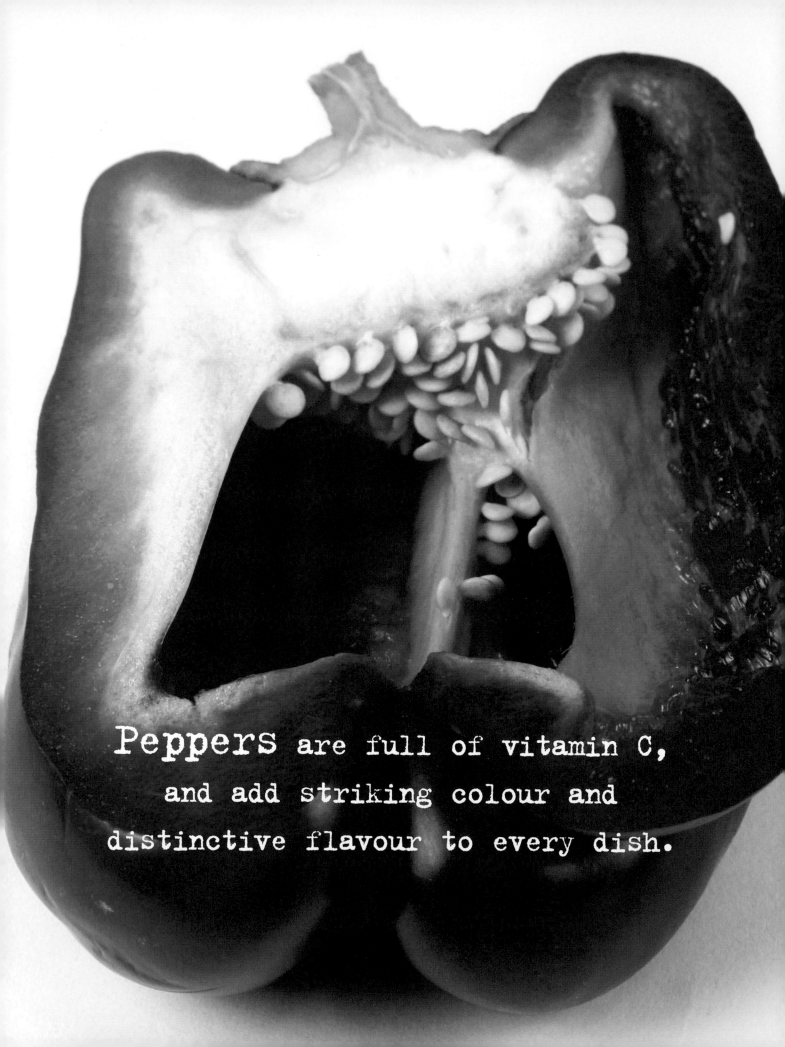

Peppers are full of vitamin C, and add striking colour and distinctive flavour to every dish.

PEPPERS STUFFED WITH MINTED RICE

Sweet roasted peppers are filled with savoury rice and topped with the sharp tang of feta cheese.

4 red peppers, cut in half lengthways, seeds removed but stalks left on
3 sun-dried tomatoes in oil, chopped, plus 2 teaspoons of the oil
150g onions, finely chopped
1–2 cloves garlic, crushed
200g long-grain white rice
450ml vegetable stock or water
4 tablespoons dry white wine
450g plum tomatoes

25g green olives, stoned and chopped
2 spring onions, finely chopped
25g pine nuts, toasted
2–3 tablespoons chopped fresh mint
Salt and black pepper
100g feta cheese, drained and crumbled

PREPARATION TIME 20–30 minutes
COOKING TIME 50–55 minutes
SERVES 4

1 Heat the oven to 200°C (400°F, gas mark 6). Place the peppers closely together, cut side up, in an ovenproof dish and bake for 20 minutes, or until softened. Remove from the oven and set aside. **2** Meanwhile, heat 2 teaspoons of oil from the jar of sun-dried tomatoes in a large nonstick saucepan and sauté the onions for 5 minutes, or until softened. Add the garlic and sun-dried tomatoes and continue cooking for a further 2 minutes, then stir in the rice. **3** Pour the stock or water and wine into the rice mixture, stir well and bring to the boil. Cover and simmer for 15–20 minutes until the liquid has been absorbed and the rice is tender. Add a little more water if the rice dries out during cooking. **4** Meanwhile, cover the tomatoes with boiling water, leave for 1 minute, then skin, deseed and chop them. Add them to the cooked rice mixture with the olives, spring onions, pine nuts and mint, season well and stir to combine. Spoon the rice into the peppers and sprinkle the feta cheese over the top. **5** Return the peppers to the top shelf of the oven and cook for a further 15 minutes, then serve.

NUTRIENTS PER SERVING KCAL 412 • CARBOHYDRATE 57g (of which 16g sugars) • PROTEIN 11g • FAT 14g (of which saturated fat 4g) • FIBRE 4g • SODIUM 735mg • SALT 1.8g • VEGETABLE PORTION 1

eggs and cheese

EGGS AND CHEESE

VEGETARIAN SCOTCH EGGS

Here's a vegetarian version of a popular Scottish speciality, using kidney beans and a delicious mixture of herbs and seeds to make a firm, tasty outer coating. Serve it with a green salad.

1 tablespoon sunflower oil
1 small onion, finely chopped
1 clove garlic, crushed
400g canned kidney beans, drained and rinsed
85g mature Cheddar cheese, grated
2 teaspoons finely chopped fresh sage
1 teaspoon sesame seeds
1 teaspoon sunflower seeds
Salt and black pepper

4 small eggs, hard-boiled, plus 1 large egg for coating
55g dried wholemeal breadcrumbs
Groundnut oil for deep-frying

PREPARATION TIME 30 minutes
COOKING TIME 15 minutes
SERVES 4

1 Heat the oil in the frying pan, add the onion and cook for 4–5 minutes until soft, then add the garlic and cook for a further minute. **2** Put the kidney beans in a blender or food processor. Add the onion and garlic, cheese, sage, sesame and sunflower seeds, and salt and pepper to taste. Purée until combined. **3** Divide the mixture into four and, using wet hands, mould each portion evenly around an egg. **4** For the coating, crack the raw egg into a small, shallow bowl and beat with a little salt. Put the breadcrumbs in a separate bowl. Toss each coated egg in the beaten egg, then in the breadcrumbs. Transfer to a plate and chill for 10–15 minutes. **5** In a deep-fat fryer, deep-fry the eggs, in 2 batches, for 1–2 minutes until golden. Drain on kitchen paper and serve hot or cold with a mustard sauce made from English mustard and sour cream.

NUTRIENTS PER SERVING KCAL 477 • CARBOHYDRATE 26g (of which 14g sugars) • PROTEIN 24g • FAT 31g (of which saturated fat 9g) • FIBRE 7g • SODIUM 756mg • SALT 1.9g • VEGETABLE PORTION 0

CREAMY CURRIED EGGS

A coconut curry sauce goes beautifully with eggs, and an aromatic vegetable pilaf is perfect alongside. This spicy dish is so well-balanced, nutritionally, that it needs no accompaniment.

20g unsalted butter
1 small onion, very finely chopped
1 garlic clove, crushed
1 tablespoon curry paste
1 can chopped tomatoes, about 200g
90ml coconut milk
2 tablespoons chopped fresh coriander
8 eggs, at room temperature

CAULIFLOWER AND PEA PILAF
1 tablespoon sunflower oil
170g small cauliflower florets
1 fresh red chilli, seeded and very finely chopped
1 cinnamon stick, halved
4 whole cloves
1 bay leaf
250g basmati rice
600ml vegetable stock
150g frozen peas
salt and pepper
sprigs of fresh coriander to garnish

TOTAL TIME 45 minutes
SERVES 4

1 Melt the butter in a non-stick saucepan and gently fry the onion for 7–8 minutes or until softened. Stir in the garlic and curry paste, and cook for a further 1 minute. Add the chopped tomatoes with their juice and simmer for 10 minutes or until fairly thick. Stir in the coconut milk and simmer for a further 5 minutes. Add the chopped coriander, and season with salt and pepper to taste. Cover and keep warm. **2** To make the pilaf, heat the oil in a heavy-based saucepan, add the cauliflower florets and cook over a moderate heat for 1–2 minutes, stirring frequently, until just beginning to colour. Stir in the chilli, cinnamon stick, cloves and bay leaf, and cook for a further 30 seconds. **3** Add the rice and stir well to mix with the vegetables and spices. Pour in the stock. Bring to the boil, then reduce the heat, cover and simmer gently for 5 minutes. Stir in the peas, cover the pan again and cook for a further 7–10 minutes or until the rice is tender and all the stock has been absorbed. Season with salt and pepper to taste. **4** While the pilaf is cooking, hard-boil the eggs. Put them into a saucepan and cover with tepid water. Bring to the boil, then reduce the heat and simmer for 7 minutes. Remove the eggs with a draining spoon and place in a bowl of cold water. When they are cool enough to handle, peel off their shells and cut them in half lengthways. **5** Arrange the egg halves on warmed serving plates and spoon over the coconut sauce. Serve with the pilaf, removing the bay leaf and whole spices first, if preferred. Garnish with sprigs of fresh coriander.

**NUTRIENTS PER SERVING KCAL 528 • CARBOHYDRATE 59g (of which 6g sugars) • PROTEIN 25g
• FAT 22g (of which saturated fat 7g) • FIBRE 3g • SODIUM 601mg • SALT 1.5g
• VEGETABLE PORTION 1**

Not just delicious and satisfying **bread** also helps to ward off intestinal diseases and lower cholesterol levels.

CHEESE AND ONION RAREBIT

Here is a richly flavoured rarebit made with mature Cheddar cheese, thickened with breadcrumbs to add texture, and spooned over thinly sliced red onions before being grilled until golden and bubbling. A spinach, apple and celery salad is the perfect partner.

90ml semi-skimmed milk
½ teaspoon mustard powder
125g well-flavoured mature Cheddar cheese, grated
40g fresh wholemeal breadcrumbs
4 thick slices wholemeal bread, about 45g each
1 small red onion, very thinly sliced

BABY SPINACH, APPLE AND CELERY SALAD
1 tablespoon walnut or hazelnut oil
2 teaspoon red wine vinegar
2 teaspoon poppy seeds
200g baby spinach leaves
2 red-skinned dessert apples, quartered, cored and sliced
2 celery sticks, sliced
salt and pepper

PREPARATION TIME 15 minutes, plus 5 minutes standing
COOKING TIME 2–3 minutes
SERVES 4

1 Preheat the grill to high. Put the milk, mustard powder and cheese in a small heavy-based saucepan and stir over a gentle heat until the cheese has melted and the mixture is smooth. Remove from the heat and stir in the breadcrumbs. Cool for 3–4 minutes, stirring occasionally, until thickened to a spreading consistency. **2** Meanwhile, arrange the slices of bread on a baking tray and toast on both sides under the grill. **3** While the bread is toasting, make the salad. Put the sunflower oil, walnut or hazelnut oil, red wine vinegar and poppy seeds into a salad bowl, and season to taste with salt and pepper. Whisk to mix. Add the spinach, apples and celery, but do not toss. **4** Top the toast with the slices of red onion, then spoon over the cheese mixture, spreading it out to cover the toast completely. Return to the grill and cook for 2–3 minutes or until the cheese mixture is golden brown and bubbling. Toss the salad and serve with the rarebits.

NUTRIENTS PER SERVING KCAL 354 • CARBOHYDRATE 33g (of which 10g sugars) • PROTEIN 16g • FAT 19g (of which saturated fat 8g) • FIBRE 5.5g • SODIUM 630mg • SALT 1.6g • VEGETABLE PORTION 1

NUTTY SPINACH AND MUSHROOM FRITATTA

This hearty omelette, packed with crunchy nuts, ribbons of spinach and tender mushrooms, can be served hot for lunch or supper or cut into thick slices for a cold packed lunch or picnic.

250g young spinach leaves
A small bunch of fresh parsley
2 tablespoons olive oil
1 small onion
350g small, closed cup mushrooms
75g roasted cashew nuts
5 medium eggs
Salt and black pepper
85g Cheddar or Italian-style premium cheese

TOTAL TIME 25 minutes
SERVES 4

1 Preheat the grill to high. Then rinse and dry the spinach and parsley and chop enough parsley to give 2 tablespoons; set aside. **2** Heat the oil in a large frying pan. Halve, peel and finely chop the onion. Fry over a moderate heat for 3–4 minutes, stirring, until soft. **3** Clean the mushrooms, quarter them, add them to the chopped onion and fry, stirring frequently, for a further 3–4 minutes. **4** Add the spinach and cook over a fairly high heat, stirring frequently, for 3–4 minutes, until the leaves have wilted and the excess liquid has evaporated. Stir in the cashews and reduce the heat to low. **5** Break the eggs into a bowl, then add 2 tablespoons of cold water and the chopped parsley. Add seasoning and beat together. **6** Pour the egg mixture into the spinach and cook for 5 minutes until the egg is just set and golden underneath, lifting the edges to let the uncooked egg run underneath. **7** Grate the cheese, sprinkle it over the top and grill for 2–3 minutes, until the fritatta is set and golden, making sure that the handle of your frying pan does not burn. Alternatively, place the fritatta on a baking tray underneath the grill.

NUTRIENTS PER SERVING KCAL 395 • CARBOHYDRATE 6g (of which 3g sugars) • PROTEIN 22g • FAT 32g (of which saturated fat 10g) • FIBRE 3g • SODIUM 356mg • SALT 0.9g • VEGETABLE PORTION 2

MOZZARELLA IN CARROZZA

A classic Italian sandwich, which literally means 'mozzarella in a carriage', makes a delicious and very quick meal. Chopped sun-dried tomatoes and fresh basil leaves enhance the flavour of the cheese, which oozes from the middle of the eggy bread.

**8 slices close-textured white bread,
  cut 1cm thick, about 325g in total**
170g mozzarella cheese, grated
**85g sun-dried tomatoes packed in oil, well
  drained and roughly chopped**
16 large fresh basil leaves
150ml semi-skimmed milk
2 large eggs, beaten
1 tablespoon extra virgin olive oil
salt and pepper

TOMATO AND ORANGE SALAD
2 oranges
6 plum tomatoes, sliced
1 teaspoon balsamic vinegar
1 garlic clove, crushed
30g stoned black olives, halved

PREPARATION TIME 15 minutes
COOKING TIME 8–10 minutes
SERVES 4

1 First make the salad. Peel and slice the oranges, working over a bowl to catch all the juice. Arrange the tomatoes and orange slices, slightly overlapping, in a shallow dish. Add the vinegar, garlic, and salt and pepper to taste to the orange juice and whisk to mix. Sprinkle this dressing over the salad. Scatter over the olives. Set aside. **2** Lay four of the slices of bread on a board or work surface. Divide the mozzarella cheese evenly among the slices. Scatter the sun-dried tomatoes on the cheese, then arrange the basil leaves over the tomatoes. Place the remaining four slices of bread on top and press down firmly. **3** Pour the milk into a shallow bowl. Add the eggs and season with salt and pepper to taste. Gently whisk together. Lay the sandwiches in the bowl, one at a time, and spoon the milk and egg mixture over so that the bread is evenly and thoroughly moistened on both sides. **4** Lightly grease a ridged cast-iron grill pan or griddle with 1½ teaspoons of the oil. Heat the pan over a moderate heat. Place two of the sandwiches in the pan and cook for 1–2 minutes on each side, turning carefully with two spatulas to hold the sandwiches together, until golden brown and crisp. **5** Remove the sandwiches from the pan and keep warm while cooking the other two sandwiches, using the remaining 1½ teaspoons of oil. Cut the sandwiches in half and serve hot, with the tomato and orange salad.

**NUTRIENTS PER SERVING KCAL 500 • CARBOHYDRATE 47g (of which 9g sugars) • PROTEIN 21g
• FAT 24g (of which saturated fat 8g) • FIBRE 3g • SODIUM 744mg • SALT 1.8g
• VEGETABLE PORTION 1**

BUCKWHEAT CRÊPES STUFFED WITH SPINACH AND RICOTTA

A creamy but light filling transforms these nutty-flavoured pancakes, popular in Normandy and Brittany, into a great dish for relaxed entertainment. Serve them with tomatoes and fresh basil.

150g plain white flour
100g buckwheat flour
Salt and black pepper
1 whole egg and 1 egg white
Sunflower oil for greasing

FOR THE FILLING
200g quark
100g half-fat cottage cheese
100g ricotta cheese

300g fresh spinach
2–4 tablespoons lemon juice
½ teaspoon grated nutmeg

TO GARNISH paprika

PREPARATION TIME 20 minutes, plus
  30 minutes standing
COOKING TIME 25 minutes
MAKES 8 crêpes

1 Bring the quark, cottage cheese and ricotta to room temperature and set aside. **2** To make the crêpes, sift the flours and 1 teaspoon of salt together. Whisk the egg and egg white together in a small bowl with 450ml of water until well blended, then gradually add the mixture to the flour, whisking well. Set aside for 30 minutes. **3** Rinse the spinach and remove any tough stalks, then put it into a saucepan, with the water still clinging to the leaves. Cover and cook for 3–4 minutes over a medium heat until it is wilted, then drain well. **4** When the spinach is cool enough to handle, squeeze out the excess water and chop it finely. Mix the cheeses and spinach together and season with the lemon juice, nutmeg, and salt and pepper to taste. **5** To cook the crêpes, heat a small nonstick frying pan over a medium-high heat. Stir the batter and check that it is thin enough to pour: if not, add water, 1 tablespoon at a time. When the pan is hot, wipe it with kitchen paper dipped in sunflower oil, then pour in 2–3 tablespoons of the batter and tilt the pan until the batter coats the base. Cook the crêpe for 1½ minutes, or until the edges begin to brown and curl up. **6** Loosen the edges gently with a thin spatula, then turn the crêpe over and cook it for a further 20-30 seconds. Do not be tempted to flip the crêpe too soon as the batter will stick to the pan, and take care not to overcook it: if the crêpe dries out it will be difficult to fold over. **7** Cook seven more crêpes in the same way, regreasing the pan when necessary. Either fill and serve each crêpe as you go along or, if you want to serve everyone at once, pile the crêpes up between sheets of kitchen paper and loosely cover with foil. **8** To serve, spread 2–3 tablespoons of the filling along the centre of each hot crêpe, then fold one side over the other. Serve the crêpes sprinkled with paprika and accompanied by tomatoes garnished with basil.

NUTRIENTS PER SERVING KCAL 180 • CARBOHYDRATE 27g (of which 3g sugars) • PROTEIN 11g • FAT 3g (of which saturated fat 1g) • FIBRE 1.5g • SODIUM 133mg • SALT 0.33g • VEGETABLE PORTION 0

ONION, FETA CHEESE AND MARJORAM PIZZAS

In this simple, thin-crust pizza, the sweetness of caramelised onions is balanced by the saltiness of feta cheese. They are delicious with a green salad at a buffet lunch.

2 teaspoons dried yeast with ¾ teaspoon sugar, or 1 sachet easy-blend yeast
250g strong plain white flour
Salt and black pepper
2 tablespoons olive oil, plus oil for greasing

FOR THE TOPPING
1kg onions, peeled and thinly sliced
1 tablespoon sugar

2 tablespoons balsamic vinegar
2 teaspoons dried marjoram
150g feta cheese, rinsed, dried and crumbled

PREPARATION TIME 40–50 minutes, plus 1 hour 30 minutes rising
COOKING TIME 35 minutes
MAKES 2 pizzas, each serving 4

1 First make the pizza dough. If using dried yeast, dissolve the sugar in 75ml of lukewarm water, then sprinkle in the yeast and set aside for 10-15 minutes until it is frothy. **2** Meanwhile, sift the flour and a pinch of salt into a large bowl and add the easy-blend yeast, if using. Make a well in the centre and add the olive oil and 125ml of lukewarm water if using easy-blend yeast, or the frothy yeast mixture and 50ml of lukewarm water. Stir with a wooden spoon to form a dough. **3** Turn out the dough onto a lightly floured work surface and knead for 5–10 minutes until it is smooth and elastic, adding extra flour, 1 tablespoon at a time, if necessary to stop it sticking; if it is too dry, add extra water, 1 tablespoon at a time. **4** Shape the dough into a ball and grease the cleaned bowl with a little oil. Put the dough into the bowl, roll it around so that it is lightly coated with oil and loosely cover the bowl with cling film. Leave the dough to rise in a warm place for 1 hour, or until it has doubled in size. **5** Meanwhile, to make the topping, bring a large pan of water to the boil. Add the onions, reduce the heat and let them simmer for 10 minutes, or until they have softened, then drain well. **6** Put the onions into a large nonstick frying pan with the sugar, balsamic vinegar, and salt to taste. Cook them over a medium-high heat, stirring, for 10 minutes, or until the liquid has reduced but not dried out completely. The sugar should have caramelised slightly and the onions should have a rich flavour. Stir in the marjoram and some black pepper and adjust the seasoning if necessary. **7** Turn out the risen dough onto a lightly floured surface, punch it down and knead it for 2–3 minutes. Return it to the bowl, cover it once more and set aside for 30 minutes for the dough to rise again. **8** Meanwhile, heat the oven to 240°C (475°F, gas mark 9). Lightly grease two baking sheets. **9** Turn out the dough, punch it down and divide it into two pieces. Shape each piece into a ball, then roll it out into a 25cm circle and place on a baking sheet. Drain off any liquid from the onions, then spread them evenly over each pizza and sprinkle with the feta cheese. **10** Bake for 12 minutes, or until the cheese has melted and the edges of the pizzas are crisp and golden. Serve them straight from the oven.

NUTRIENTS PER SERVING KCAL 237 • CARBOHYDRATE 37g (of which 10g sugars) • PROTEIN 8g • FAT 8g (of which saturated fat 3g) • FIBRE 3g • SODIUM 275mg • SALT 0.7g • VEGETABLE PORTION 1

PIZZA TART WITH CHERRY TOMATOES

A cheese-flavoured pizza dough makes a delicious case for a ricotta cheese and herb filling topped with sweet cherry tomatoes and black olives. Serve with a salad of mixed leaves and poppy, pumpkin and sunflower seeds, toasted to bring out their flavour.

CHEESY PIZZA DOUGH
170g strong white (bread) flour
½ teaspoon easy-blend dried yeast
30g Italian-style premium cheese, freshly grated
120ml tepid water
2 tablespoons extra virgin olive oil

RICOTTA FILLING
170g ricotta cheese
2 teaspoons chopped fresh oregano
1 tablespoon chopped parsley
250g cherry tomatoes, halved
50g stoned black olives
2 tablespoons balsamic vinegar
1 small sprig of fresh rosemary
1 garlic clove, crushed
salt and pepper

LEAFY SALAD WITH MIXED SEEDS
50g pumpkin seeds
50g sunflower seeds
2 teaspoons poppy seeds
1 teaspoon soy sauce
2 teaspoons sunflower oil
1 teaspoon walnut oil
1 teaspoon cider vinegar
150g mixed salad leaves, such as baby
    spinach, rocket and oak leaf lettuce

PREPARATION TIME 35–40 minutes, plus
    1 hour rising
COOKING TIME 15–20 minutes
SERVES 4

Tomatoes are a real superfood. Lycopene, the pigment that turns tomatoes red, may help to prevent some forms of cancer.

1 To make the dough, sift the flour and ½ teaspoon of salt into a bowl, and stir in the yeast and grated cheese. Make a well in the centre. Add the water and 1 tablespoon of the oil, and mix to form a dough. Add a bit more water if needed. **2** Turn out onto a lightly floured surface and knead for 10 minutes or until smooth and elastic. Return the dough to the bowl, cover with cling film and leave in a warm place to rise for about 1 hour or until doubled in size. **3** Preheat the oven to 220°C (425°F, gas mark 7) and place a baking sheet inside to heat. Knock back the dough, then turn it out onto the floured surface and knead briefly. Roll out to a 30cm round about 5mm thick. Use to line a lightly oiled, loose-bottomed, shallow 25cm tart tin, leaving the edges ragged and slightly hanging over the edge of the tin. **4** Mix the ricotta with the oregano and parsley, and season with salt and pepper to taste. Spread evenly in the dough case. Arrange the tomatoes, cut side up, and the olives on top. **5** Gently heat the balsamic vinegar with the remaining tablespoon of olive oil, the rosemary and garlic in a small pan. Bubble for 1–2 minutes or until it has reduced a little, then drizzle over the tomatoes and olives. **6** Place the tart tin on the preheated baking sheet. Bake for 15–20 minutes or until the case is crisp and golden brown and the tomatoes are slightly caramelised. **7** Meanwhile, make the salad. In a small non-stick frying pan, toast the pumpkin, sunflower and poppy seeds over a moderate heat for 2–3 minutes, turning frequently. Sprinkle over the soy sauce and toss together. The seeds will stick together initially, but will separate as the mixture dries. Remove from the heat. **8** Whisk together the sunflower and walnut oils, vinegar and seasoning to taste in a salad bowl. Add the salad leaves, sprinkle with the toasted seeds and toss together. **9** Remove the tart from the tin and cut it into four wedges. Serve hot, with the salad.

NUTRIENTS PER SERVING KCAL 490 • CARBOHYDRATE 41g (of which 4g sugars) • PROTEIN 18g • FAT 30g (of which saturated fat 7.5g) • FIBRE 4g • SODIUM 327mg • SALT 0.8g • VEGETABLE PORTION 1

LEEK AND CHEDDAR CHEESE TART

This tasty tart with leeks, cheese and a dash of mustard looks as pretty as a picture. Save time by choosing trimmed, cleaned leeks and using ready-made puff pastry.

7–8 slim leeks, about 950g in total
Salt and black pepper
250g fresh puff pastry
1 tablespoon Dijon mustard
1 medium egg
50g Cheddar cheese

TOTAL TIME 30 minutes
SERVES 4

1 Preheat the oven to 230°C (450°F, gas mark 7). Put a kettle of water on to boil. **2** If necessary, trim the leeks to about 18cm and rinse them. Arrange them in a single layer in a wide saucepan or frying pan, pour on the boiling water from the kettle, add a pinch of salt, return to the boil, reduce the heat and simmer, covered, for 6–8 minutes. **3** While they are cooking, roll out the puff pastry on a lightly floured surface to a 25cm square, then transfer the pastry square onto a baking sheet. **4** Cut a 1cm strip of pastry from each of the four sides. Dampen the area round the edge of the square with water and trim the pastry strips to fit on top of the dampened edges, so that they look like a picture frame; press them lightly into place. **5** Drain the leeks and cool them under cold running water. Drain again, then wrap them in a folded tea towel and press them gently to remove any remaining moisture. **6** Arrange the leeks inside the pastry case and brush them with the mustard. Break the egg into a small bowl and beat it lightly, then brush the border of the tart with the beaten egg. Grate the Cheddar cheese and spread it evenly over the top of the leeks. **7** Bake on the top shelf of the oven for 15 minutes, or until the pastry is risen and golden and the cheese has melted and is bubbling. Then remove it from the oven and cut it into quarters with a serrated-edged knife. Serve hot or warm.

NUTRIENTS PER SERVING KCAL 360 • CARBOHYDRATE 30g (of which 6g sugars) • PROTEIN 12g • FAT 22g (of which saturated fat 11g) • FIBRE 5g • SODIUM 310mg • SALT 0.8g • VEGETABLE PORTION 2

CHILLIED POTATO AND LEEK QUICHE

If you love quiche but are tired of the usual fillings, here's a new idea to whet your appetite. A vibrant green layer of peppery rocket is sandwiched between sliced potatoes and leeks in a cheese-flavoured custard, and the crisp pastry case is speckled with hot chilli and fragrant thyme.

SUNFLOWER OIL SHORTCRUST PASTRY
170g plain flour
2 fresh red chillies, seeded and finely chopped
2 teaspoons chopped fresh thyme
1 egg
4 tablespoons sunflower oil
1 tablespoon tepid water

POTATO AND LEEK FILLING
350g waxy new potatoes, scrubbed
250g leeks, cut into 1cm slices
55g Emmental cheese, grated
2 tablespoons snipped fresh chives
55g rocket, roughly chopped
2 eggs
150ml semi-skimmed milk
salt and pepper

PREPARATION TIME 30 minutes, plus
  30 minutes resting
COOKING TIME 40–45 minutes
SERVES 4

1 To make the pastry, sift the flour and a pinch of salt into a bowl. Stir in the chillies and thyme, then make a well in the centre. Whisk together the egg, oil and water, add to the dry ingredients and mix together with a fork to make a dough. **2** Turn out the dough onto a lightly floured surface and knead for a few seconds until smooth. Put into a bowl, cover with a damp tea-towel and leave to rest for about 30 minutes before rolling out. **3** Meanwhile, make the filling. Cook the potatoes in boiling water for 10–12 minutes or until almost tender. Steam the leeks over the potatoes for 6–7 minutes, or cook them in a separate pan of boiling water for 4–5 minutes, until tender. Drain thoroughly and leave until cool enough to handle. **4** Preheat the oven to 200°C (400°F, gas mark 6) and put a baking sheet in to heat. Roll out the pastry dough thinly and use to line a 20cm round, loose-bottomed, fluted flan tin about 3cm deep. Scatter half the cheese over the bottom of the case. **5** Thickly slice the warm potatoes and toss with the leeks, the remaining cheese, the chives, and salt and pepper to taste. Arrange half of the potato and leek mixture in a layer in the pastry case. Scatter over the chopped rocket, then spread the rest of the potato and leek mixture on top. **6** Lightly beat the eggs together in a jug. Heat the milk to just below boiling point, then add to the eggs, whisking gently to mix. **7** Place the tin on the hot baking sheet and carefully pour the warm egg custard into the pastry case. Bake for 10 minutes, then reduce the oven temperature to 180°C (350°F, gas mark 4). Bake for a further 30–35 minutes or until the filling is lightly set. Leave in the tin for 5 minutes before removing. Serve warm with a tomato and red onion salad.

NUTRIENTS PER SERVING KCAL 459 • CARBOHYDRATE 51g (of which 5g sugars) • PROTEIN 17g • FAT 22g (of which saturated fat 6g) • FIBRE 4g • SODIUM 185mg • SALT 0.47g • VEGETABLE PORTION 0

The tender spears of lightly boiled or steamed **asparagus** are a delicacy best enjoyed with the freshest seasonal produce.

ASPARAGUS FLAN

Asparagus adds vitamins and body to this creamy, elegant flan; roasting the vegetable enhances its delicate flavour. Serve it warm or cold, with a tomato and chive salad to add a colour contrast.

175g fresh asparagus, trimmed
3 teaspoons olive oil
6 spring onions, trimmed and cut into
  7.5cm lengths
2 eggs
100g fresh goat's cheese
70g curd cheese
4 tablespoons milk
Salt and black pepper

FOR THE PASTRY
1 egg yolk
½ teaspoon sugar
280g plain white flour
½ teaspoon salt
115g butter, cut into small pieces

PREPARATION TIME 35 minutes
COOKING TIME 35 minutes
SERVES 6

1 Heat the oven to 190°C (375°F, gas mark 5). For the pastry, put the egg yolk, sugar and 5 tablespoons cold water in a small bowl and beat. Sift the flour and salt into a separate bowl. Rub the butter into the flour until the mixture resembles fine breadcrumbs. **2** Make a well in the centre of the flour mixture and add the egg yolk mixture. Using the back of a knife, stir until the mixture holds together, adding a little more cold water if necessary. Knead lightly, then roll out the pastry on a floured surface and use to line a 20cm flan dish. Prick the base all over with a fork and refrigerate for about 30 minutes. **3** Bake the pastry for 6–8 minutes until pale but firm. Remove from the oven and set aside. **4** If the asparagus spears are thick, cut them in half lengthways. Put in a shallow ovenproof dish and pour over 2 teaspoons oil. Roast in the oven for 10 minutes, turning once, until tender. **5** Heat the remaining teaspoon of oil in a small frying pan, add the spring onions and cook over a medium heat until slightly softened. **6** Put the eggs, goat's cheese, curd cheese and milk in a bowl and beat. Add salt and pepper to taste. Pour the egg mixture into the flan dish and arrange the asparagus and spring onions on top. Bake for 18–20 minutes until golden. Serve immediately or allow it to cool and serve cold.

NUTRIENTS PER SERVING KCAL 480 • CARBOHYDRATE 38g (of which 3g sugars) • PROTEIN 12g • FAT 32g (of which saturated fat 18g) • FIBRE 2g • SODIUM 452mg • SALT 1.1g • VEGETABLE PORTION 0

KIDNEY BEAN AND VEGETABLE GRATIN

Raisins, chillies and fresh herbs add interesting flavours to a rich, warming casserole of rice, vegetables and beans, topped with grilled cheese and served with Greek yoghurt.

3 tablespoons virgin olive oil
1 medium onion
2 medium sticks celery
2 cloves garlic
1 medium red pepper
125g seedless raisins
A pinch of dried oregano
A pinch of dried crushed red chillies
1 teaspoon ground cumin
Salt and black pepper
400g canned chopped tomatoes
175g broccoli
A handful of fresh coriander
420g canned kidney beans
275g canned cooked 'Microwave' rice
125g frozen sweetcorn
70g Italian-style premium cheese

TO SERVE
200g natural Greek yoghurt, or 200ml soured cream, fresh crusty bread

TIME 30 minutes
SERVES 4

1 Put a kettle of water on to boil. Heat the oil in a large, heavy-based saucepan over a very low heat. **2** Peel and chop the onion, rinse and thinly slice the celery and peel and crush the garlic. Add them to the oil; fry gently for 5 minutes. **3** Rinse, deseed and chop the pepper and add it to the pan with the raisins, oregano, crushed chillies and cumin and fry for 2 minutes. **4** Add salt and pepper, the canned tomatoes and 5 tablespoons of water. Bring to the boil, reduce the heat, and simmer for 5 minutes. **5** Rinse the broccoli, cut it into florets, put them into a saucepan and cover with boiling water. Bring back to the boil, cook for 2 minutes, then drain and set aside. **6** Preheat the grill to medium. Rinse and chop enough coriander to give 4 tablespoons and set aside. **7** Drain and rinse the kidney beans and add them to the vegetable mixture, with the canned rice and sweetcorn. Return to the boil, lower the heat and simmer for 2 minutes. Add the broccoli and heat for a further minute. **8** Remove the pan from the heat, then stir in the coriander and grate the cheese over the top. Grill the gratin for 5–6 minutes to melt the cheese. **9** Serve accompanied by yoghurt or soured cream and crusty bread.

NUTRIENTS PER SERVING KCAL 625 • CARBOHYDRATE 85g (of which 36g sugars) • PROTEIN 26g • FAT 22g (of which saturated fat 8g) • FIBRE 10g • SODIUM 629mg • SALT 1.6g • VEGETABLE PORTION 2

CHEDDAR AND BROCCOLI STRATA

A satisfying savoury pudding is made up of layers of bread and vegetables with a cheesy egg custard topping. Served with a quick home-made tomato sauce, it is a tasty and nutritious dish. A leafy salad could be served alongside.

15g butter
4 shallots, finely chopped
250g broccoli, cut into small florets
170g fine green beans, halved
1 can sweetcorn kernels, about 200g, drained
9 thick slices of white bread, about 400g in total, crusts removed and slices cut in half
4 eggs
600ml semi-skimmed milk
2 tablespoons snipped fresh chives
2 tablespoons chopped parsley
85g mature Cheddar cheese, grated
salt and pepper

TOMATO SAUCE
1 tablespoon extra virgin olive oil
1 red onion, finely chopped
2 garlic cloves, crushed
2 cans chopped tomatoes with herbs, about 400g each
2 tablespoons tomato purée

PREPARATION TIME 30 minutes, plus 30 minutes standing
COOKING TIME 1 hour
SERVES 6

1 Melt the butter in a frying pan, add the shallots and cook gently for about 7 minutes or until softened. Meanwhile, cook the broccoli and green beans in a saucepan of boiling water for 4 minutes or until just tender. Drain well, then stir into the shallots together with the sweetcorn. Season to taste. **2** Arrange six of the halved bread slices side by side in a lightly greased, deep ovenproof dish. Top with half of the broccoli mixture. Repeat the layers of bread and broccoli mixture, then finish with a layer of bread. **3** Whisk together the eggs, milk, chives and parsley, and season with salt and pepper to taste. Pour the mixture over the layered bread and vegetables, and sprinkle the cheese on top. Set aside for 30 minutes, to allow the bread to soak up some of the liquid. Preheat the oven to 180°C (350°F, gas mark 4). **4** Meanwhile, make the tomato sauce. Heat the oil in a saucepan, add the onion and garlic, and cook over a moderate heat for 5 minutes. Stir in the tomatoes, with their juice, and the tomato purée. Bring to the boil, then reduce the heat, cover and simmer for 15 minutes. Uncover the pan, increase the heat slightly and cook for a further 5–10 minutes, stirring occasionally, until the sauce has thickened slightly. **5** Bake the pudding for 1 hour or until set, puffy and golden brown. Just before the cooking time is up, warm the sauce gently. Spoon the strata onto hot serving plates and serve with the tomato sauce.

NUTRIENTS PER SERVING KCAL 439 • CARBOHYDRATE 53g (of which 1g sugars) • PROTEIN 23g • FAT 17g (of which saturated fat 7g) • FIBRE 5g • SODIUM 1012mg • SALT 2.5g • VEGETABLE PORTION 3

des

and other sweet things

Serts

DESSERTS
AND OTHER SWEET THINGS

BAKED APPLES GLAZED WITH PORT

For easy entertaining, this luscious dessert of richly glazed apples with a prune filling can be prepared in advance and then baked just before serving.

4 large dessert apples, cored
175g ready-to-eat stoned prunes, chopped
20g soft dark brown sugar
450ml port
Finely grated zest of 1 lemon
Finely grated zest of 1 orange
5cm cinnamon stick
2–3 cloves, optional

1 teaspoon icing sugar

TO SERVE low-fat fromage frais or half-fat
  Greek yoghurt, optional

PREPARATION TIME 20 minutes
COOKING TIME 1hour–1 hour 15 minutes
SERVES 4

1 Heat the oven to 220°C (425°F, gas mark 7). **2** Place one of the apples upright and make deep cuts from the top down through it to within 2cm of the bottom to divide it into eight equal segments. Do the same with the remaining apples, then place them close together in a shallow ovenproof dish. **3** Gently push a quarter of the prunes into the centre of each apple – they do not have to go all the way down. Sprinkle the apples with the brown sugar and pour the port over them. Add the lemon and orange zests, cinnamon stick and cloves, if using, to the dish. **4** Bake, uncovered, for 15 minutes, then reduce the temperature to 180°C (350°F, gas mark 4) and bake for a further 45 minutes–1 hour, basting the apples with the port every 10-15 minutes until they have softened but not broken up and the port has reduced to a syrupy consistency. **5** Serve the apples on individual plates with the port sauce spooned over them. Sift a little icing sugar over the top and accompany with fromage frais or yoghurt, if you like.

NUTRIENTS PER SERVING KCAL 363 • CARBOHYDRATE 60g (of which 50g sugars) • PROTEIN 2g • NO FAT • FIBRE 5g • SODIUM 14mg • SALT trace • FRUIT PORTION 2

Dried **figs** have six times the calories of fresh figs, but they are a richer source of fibre and minerals.

GRILLED FIGS

A gorgeous dessert featuring plump fresh figs, scented with rosewater and oozing with beautiful pink juices.

15g butter at room temperature
8 large fresh figs
1 lemon
A few drops of rosewater, optional

6 tablespoons caster sugar
6 tablespoons crème fraîche

TOTAL TIME 20 minutes
SERVES 4

1 Preheat the grill to its highest setting for 10 minutes. Lightly butter a small, flameproof dish. **2** Rinse, dry and remove the stalks from the figs, then cut them in half. **3** Squeeze the lemon juice into a small bowl and add the rosewater, if using. Toss the figs in the scented juice then arrange them, cut sides down, in one layer in the buttered dish. Sprinkle the skins liberally with 3 tablespoons of the sugar. **4** Place under the hot grill and cook for 3–4 minutes. Turn them over, sprinkle the cut sides with the remaining sugar and grill them for a further 2–3 minutes. Serve piping hot, bathed in their pink juices, with the crème fraîche.

NUTRIENTS PER SERVING KCAL 266 • CARBOHYDRATE 38g (of which 38g sugars) • PROTEIN 2.5g • FAT 12.5g (of which saturated fat 8g) • FIBRE 2g • SODIUM 33mg • SALT trace • FRUIT PORTION 1

SPICED SEASONAL FRUIT SALAD

Use any soft fruit in season for this slightly piquant medley of flavours, a perfect follow-on to a spicy main course. You can add to the glamour of this dish by using lesser-known exotic fruits.

1 large mango
125g seedless black grapes, cut in half
125g seedless green grapes, cut in half
125g peaches, skinned, stoned and sliced
125g strawberries, hulled and cut in half or
  into quarters, according to size
25g unsweetened desiccated coconut
30g caster sugar

A pinch of cayenne pepper
A pinch of mustard powder
Salt

PREPARATION TIME 20 minutes, plus 1 hour,
  or overnight, chilling
SERVES 4

1 Peel the mango, cut away the flesh and thinly slice it. **2** Put the mango into a large mixing bowl and add the black and green grapes, peaches and strawberries. **3** Finely grind the coconut in a spice mill or with a pestle and mortar. Add the sugar, cayenne pepper, mustard and a pinch of salt and mix well. **4** Add the coconut mixture to the fruit, stir well, cover and place in the refrigerator to chill for at least 1 hour, or overnight, to allow the flavours to blend and mature.

NUTRIENTS PER SERVING KCAL 160 • CARBOHYDRATE 31g (of which 28g sugars) • PROTEIN 2g • FAT 4g (of which saturated fat 3g) • FIBRE 3g • SODIUM 6mg • SALT trace • FRUIT PORTION 2

HOT SPICED PEACHES WITH MASCARPONE

The heat of a fresh red chilli brings out the exquisite sweetness of the peaches in this surprising, spicy dessert, while sweetened mascarpone cheese makes a refreshing alternative to cream.

125g caster sugar
2 star anise
1cm stick cinnamon
1 fresh red chilli
2 thin slices fresh ginger

1 lemon
1kg firm but ripe peaches
175g mascarpone cheese

TIME 25 minutes
SERVES 4

1 Put a kettle of water on to boil. Pour 150ml of water into a large saucepan and add 115g of the caster sugar, the star anise, cinnamon, fresh red chilli and the ginger. Stir over a moderate heat until the sugar has dissolved, then bring to the boil. **2** Wash any wax off the lemon, pare off three thin strips of rind, add them to the sugar syrup, then reduce the heat and simmer. **3** Cut the peaches in half and remove the stones, put them into a bowl and cover with boiling water. Leave for 1–2 minutes then drain and peel off their skins. Cut each half into 4–6 slices, and add them to the sugar syrup. **4** Bring the peaches to the boil, then reduce the heat and simmer gently for 5 minutes, or until they are just softened. **5** Meanwhile, stir the remaining sugar into the mascarpone. Squeeze the juice from the lemon. **6** Remove the spiced peaches from the heat, then add the lemon juice. Transfer into individual dishes and serve, warm or cold, with a little syrup and the mascarpone.

NUTRIENTS PER SERVING KCAL 403 • CARBOHYDRATE 54g (of which 54g sugars) • PROTEIN 4g • FAT 21g (of which saturated fat 13g) • FIBRE 4g • SODIUM 30mg • SALT trace • FRUIT PORTION 2

BARBECUED FRUIT

What could be nicer, to end a barbecue, that a skewerful of delicious barbecued fruit? The icing sugar coating turns a delicious chewy brown, and you can choose whichever fruits are in season.

Grated zest of ½ lemon and juice of 1 lemon
4 tablespoons Cointreau or brandy
2–3 tablespoons honey or brown sugar
1 tablespoon bitters, such as Angostura, optional
1 pineapple, peeled and cored
250g strawberries, hulled
2 tablespoons icing sugar

TO DECORATE
sifted icing sugar

PREPARATION TIME 15 minutes, plus 1hour, or overnight, marinating
COOKING TIME 8–10 minutes
SERVES 4

1 In a china or glass bowl, stir together the lemon juice, liqueur and honey or sugar, adding the bitters, if using. **2** Cut the pineapple into 2.5cm cubes and add them to the marinade, then add the strawberries. Stir well, taking care not to break up the fruit, then cover and refrigerate for at least 1 hour, or overnight. **3** Lift the strawberries and pineapple from the marinade, reserving the liquid, and thread them alternately onto eight skewers. **4** Dust the fruit with 1 tablespoon of icing sugar, then place the skewers on the barbecue, sugared side down, and cook for 4–5 minutes. Remove from the barbecue, dust the other side of the fruit with the remaining sugar and barbecue again, sugared side down. **5** Divide the skewers between four plates and drizzle the marinade over. To decorate, sift a little icing sugar over each, then serve.

NUTRIENTS PER SERVING KCAL 180 • CARBOHYDRATE 37g (of which 32g sugars) • PROTEIN 1g • NO FAT • FIBRE 2.5g • SODIUM 8mg • SALT trace • FRUIT PORTION 1

Pears hardly ever cause allergies and are full of natural sugars, so they provide safe, instant energy – deliciously.

BAKED ALMOND PEARS

Quartered pears are baked in a glorious fruit syrup and topped with almond flavoured biscuits or crisp, browned, roasted almonds, to add a crunchy texture.

50g butter, at room temperature
1 tablespoon caster sugar
4 large, firm, ripe pears
4 tablespoons white wine or orange juice
85g apricot jam or 2 tablespoons honey
6 Amaretti biscuits or 70g blanched almonds

TO SERVE cream or natural Greek yoghurt

TOTAL TIME 30 minutes
SERVES 4

1 Preheat the oven to 200°C (400°F, gas mark 6). Grease a shallow, round ovenproof dish with half the butter and sprinkle the caster sugar evenly over the top to coat the butter. **2** Peel the pears and halve them, then cut them lengthways into slices about 1cm thick. Arrange the slices in a single, overlapping layer in the bottom of the dish. **3** Mix the wine or orange juice with the apricot jam or honey and pour the mixture over the pears. **4** Crush the Amaretti biscuits with a rolling pin or finely chop the almonds. Sprinkle them over the pears. Dot the remaining butter evenly over the pears. Bake in the oven for 15–20 minutes, until the pears have softened and the biscuits or nuts are lightly browned. Serve with cream or Greek yoghurt.

NUTRIENTS PER SERVING KCAL 300 • CARBOHYDRATE 25g (of which 25g sugars) • PROTEIN 4g • FAT 20g (of which saturated fat 7g) • FIBRE 4.5g • SODIUM 87mg • SALT 0.2g • FRUIT PORTION 1

CINNAMON PINEAPPLE WITH MALIBU

Pineapple in syrup is enhanced with a coconut-flavoured liqueur for a tropical dessert.

25g glacé cherries, halved, rinsed and dried
75ml Malibu, or other coconut-flavoured
  liqueur
1.3kg pineapple
5cm cinnamon stick, halved
2 star anise
75g dark brown sugar
25g seedless raisins

TO GARNISH
sprigs of fresh mint

PREPARATION TIME 15–20 minutes, plus 45
  minutes cooling and 30 minutes chilling
COOKING TIME 30–40 minutes
SERVES 4

1 Put the glacé cherries into a bowl, pour 30ml of liqueur over them, mix well and set aside.
2 Slice off both ends of the pineapple. Peel it with a sharp knife and, using a small knife, remove the 'eyes'. Cut the flesh into quarters lengthways. Remove the fibrous core from each quarter and cut the flesh into bite-size pieces. **3** To make the syrup, put 450ml of water into a saucepan and bring to the boil. Add the pineapple, cinnamon, star anise and sugar and stir until the sugar has dissolved. Return to the boil, reduce the heat, cover and simmer for 8–10 minutes until the pineapple is cooked, but still firm. **4** Remove the pan from the heat and use a slotted spoon to transfer the pineapple to a bowl, squeezing the chunks to remove excess liquid. **5** Add the raisins to the syrup, return it to the heat and simmer for 15–20 minutes until it has reduced by a quarter. Stir in the remaining liqueur and continue simmering for 1 minute. Remove the pan from the heat and discard the cinnamon. **6** Stir the cherries into the syrup, then spoon the mixture over the pineapple. Cool and serve chilled, or at room temperature, garnished with mint.

NUTRIENTS PER SERVING KCAL 293 • CARBOHYDRATE 64g (of which 64g sugars) • PROTEIN 1.5g • NO FAT • FIBRE 4g • SODIUM 19mg • SALT trace • FRUIT PORTION 2

STRAWBERRY CLOUDS

Crushed strawberries mixed into a yoghurt and vanilla meringue are a light-as-air treat.

250g fresh strawberries
70g caster sugar
2 large egg whites
250g Greek yoghurt, chilled
½ teaspoon natural vanilla extract

TOTAL TIME 20 minutes
SERVES 4

1 Rinse and dry the strawberries and hull them, reserving 4 whole ones for decoration. Put the hulled strawberries into a bowl, sprinkle with 1 tablespoon of the sugar and crush them with a fork. **2** In a large, dry mixing bowl, whisk the egg whites until they form a soft peak, then gradually add the remaining caster sugar, whisking well after each addition, to make a stiff meringue. **3** Add the yoghurt and the vanilla extract to the meringue and gently fold them in with a metal spoon. **4** Fold the mashed strawberries and their juice into the yoghurt mixture. Be careful not to mix them in too vigorously, as the light, airy texture will be lost. **5** Spoon the meringue into four 200ml glasses and decorate with the reserved strawberries. Serve them immediately, or chill for 2–3 hours before serving.

NUTRIENTS PER SERVING KCAL 165 • **CARBOHYDRATE 23g (of which 23g sugars)** • **PROTEIN 6g** • **FAT 6g (of which saturated fat 3g)** • **FIBRE 0.7g** • **SODIUM 76mg** • **SALT 0.19g** • **FRUIT PORTION 0**

Blackcurrants have four times as much vitamin C as an orange. Drink their goodness in a juice or use as a fruity cheesecake topping.

BLACKCURRANT FOOL WITH ALMOND SHORTIES

Popular since the 17th century, fools are best made with sharp fruits. Victorian cooks favoured gooseberries, but blackcurrants make a beautiful purple coloured pudding.

1 tablespoon plain flour
1 egg yolk
4 tablespoons sugar
200ml semi-skimmed milk
350g blackcurrants, stems removed
450g Greek-style yoghurt

FOR THE ALMOND SHORTIES
85g butter, softened, plus extra for greasing

40g light muscovado sugar
¼ teaspoon almond extract
115g plain wholemeal flour
16 blanched almonds, cut into slivers

PREPARATION TIME 45 minutes, plus 4 hours
   cooling and chilling
COOKING TIME 15 minutes
SERVES 4

1 Put the flour and egg yolk into a small bowl with 3 tablespoons of the sugar. Stir in a little milk to make a smooth paste. **2** Heat the remaining milk in a saucepan until almost boiling, then stir it into the paste. Return the mixture to the pan and bring to the boil, stirring continuously. Simmer for 3 minutes, stirring, until thickened and smooth. Pour into a large bowl and cover the surface with cling film. **3** Put the blackcurrants, remaining sugar and 1 tablespoon water into a small saucepan and bring to the boil. Remove from the heat, cool slightly, then purée in a blender or food processor. Pass the mixture through a fine sieve, then stir it into the custard. Cover with cling film and leave to cool. **4** When the blackcurrant mixture is cool, fold in the yoghurt, then divide among four serving glasses. Chill for at least 3 hours. **5** Meanwhile, to make the almond shorties, heat the oven to 160°C (325°F, gas mark 3) and lightly grease a large baking sheet. Cream the butter with the sugar and almond extract until very soft, then mix in the flour. **6** Divide the dough into 16 balls, about the size of prunes. Flatten each into a 4cm round on the greased baking sheet, placing them slightly apart to allow room to spread. Lightly press a few slivered almonds into the top of each. **7** Bake for 8–10 minutes until browned and firm. Leave on the baking sheet for 2–3 minutes, until firm enough to lift without crumbling. Transfer to a wire rack to cool. Serve the fools with the almond shorties.

NUTRIENTS PER SERVING OF FOOL KCAL 284 • CARBOHYDRATE 32g (of which 29g sugars)
• PROTEIN 10g • FAT 14g (of which saturated fat 8g) • FIBRE 3g • SODIUM 101mg • SALT 0.25g
• FRUIT PORTION 1
NUTRIENTS PER ALMOND SHORTIE KCAL 100 • CARBOHYDRATE 7g (of which 3g sugars)
• PROTEIN 2g • FAT 7g (of which saturated fat 3g) • FIBRE 1g • SODIUM 34mg • SALT trace
• FRUIT PORTION 0

RASPBERRIES WITH OATS

Crunchy muesli with raisins and almonds makes a substantial partner for soft, sweet raspberries.

350g raspberries
2 tablespoons caster sugar
500g organic, natural bio yoghurt
150g muesli, or crunchy oat breakfast cereal
  with honey, raisins and almonds
1 tablespoon runny honey

TO DECORATE a little extra honey or muesli or
  breakfast cereal

TIME 10 minutes
SERVES 4

1 Put the raspberries and sugar into a bowl, mix and set aside. **2** In another bowl, mix the natural yoghurt with the muesli or breakfast cereal. Add the honey, stirring it in lightly, so the mixture is streaky. **3** Divide two-thirds of the mixture among four wide 225ml glasses. Top with the raspberries, then add the remaining mixture. Drizzle a little honey over the top, or sprinkle with muesli or cereal. **4** If it is served immediately, this dessert has a crunchy texture, but if you prefer a softer, creamier texture, chill it for 3–4 hours before serving.

NUTRIENTS PER SERVING KCAL 318 • CARBOHYDRATE 52g (of which 37g sugars) • PROTEIN 14g • FAT 7g (of which saturated fat 3g) • FIBRE 5g • SODIUM 121mg • SALT 0.3g • FRUIT PORTION 1

RHUBARB, ORANGE AND GINGER CRUMBLE

Aromatic ginger and tangy orange liven up this warm, fruity dish with a crisp, oaty topping.

1 large orange
450g rhubarb, sliced into 2.5cm pieces
2 teaspoons chopped stem ginger
1–2 tablespoons caster sugar

FOR THE CRUMBLE
125g plain white flour

75g half-fat butter, chilled and diced
25g demerara sugar
50g porridge oats

PREPARATION TIME 15 minutes
COOKING TIME 40–45 minutes
SERVES 4

1 Heat the oven to 190°C (375°F, gas mark 5). Finely grate 1 teaspoon of orange zest and set it aside. Then peel the orange, removing all the pith, and divide the flesh into segments, cutting any large ones in half. **2** Place the orange segments in a pie dish and add the rhubarb, stem ginger and caster sugar to taste. Cover the dish with foil and bake for 15 minutes. **3** Meanwhile, prepare the crumble. Place the flour, butter and demerara sugar in a bowl and combine with your fingertips until the mixture resembles breadcrumbs, or whizz them for 10–15 seconds in a food processor. Stir in the oats and the reserved orange zest. **4** Uncover the fruit and sprinkle the crumble topping over them. Return the dish to the oven, uncovered, and bake for 25–30 minutes until the topping is crisp and golden. **5** Allow the crumble to cool slightly, then serve with hot custard. If you prefer to make it in advance, it is just as delicious served chilled.

NUTRIENTS PER SERVING KCAL 306 • CARBOHYDRATE 52g (of which 19g sugars) • PROTEIN 7g • FAT 9g (of which saturated fat 2g) • FIBRE 4g • SODIUM 133mg • SALT 0.3g • FRUIT PORTION 1

MANGO SORBET WITH TROPICAL FRUIT SALAD

A rich mango and coconut sorbet complements this delightful combination of exotic fruits.

FOR THE SORBET
125g caster sugar
Juice of ½ lemon
500g canned mango pieces in syrup, drained
2 tablespoons creamed coconut, crumbled
2 egg whites

FOR THE FRUIT SALAD
1 mango, peeled, stoned and sliced
1 papaya, peeled, deseeded and diced
2 small bananas, sliced
1 star fruit, tough ribs peeled off, then sliced
250g pineapple, peeled, cored and cut into
    wedges
Juice of 2 limes or 1 large lemon

TO GARNISH 4 teaspoons shredded or
    desiccated coconut

**PREPARATION TIME 20 minutes, plus
    15 minutes cooling and at least
    4½ hours freezing**
COOKING TIME 10 minutes
SERVES 4

1 Put the sugar and 250ml of water into a small saucepan and bring the mixture to the boil, stirring until the sugar has dissolved. Reduce the heat and simmer for 5 minutes to make a syrup. Strain the lemon juice into the syrup, then set it aside for 15 minutes to cool. **2** Purée the syrup, canned mango and coconut in a food processor, or with a hand-held mixer, to make about 800ml. Pour the mixture into a freezerproof container, cover and freeze for 2 hours, or until it is just firm. (Use the fast-freeze setting if your freezer has one.) **3** When the mango mixture is frozen, whisk the egg whites until they form soft peaks. Scrape the mango mixture with a fork to form crystals, then use a whisk to beat in the egg whites, making sure they are well mixed. Return the sorbet to the freezer and freeze for 1 hour 30 minutes. **4** Remove the sorbet from the freezer and whisk it again. Press it down with a spatula and return it to the freezer for a further hour, or until it is firm. **5** When the sorbet is almost frozen, prepare the fruit for the salad and put it in a bowl. Add the lime or lemon juice and gently toss the fruit in it, then set the salad aside. **6** Heat a heavy-based nonstick frying pan and dry-fry the coconut for between 30 seconds and a minute, stirring, until it is lightly browned around the edges. **7** Serve the fruit salad with two scoops of sorbet per person, topped with the coconut. Any remaining sorbet will keep, frozen, for three months.

NUTRIENTS PER SERVING KCAL 367 • CARBOHYDRATE 82g (of which 78g sugars) • PROTEIN 4g • FAT 5g (of which saturated fat 3g) • FIBRE 4g • SODIUM 45mg • SALT 0.1g • FRUIT PORTION 2

HOT FRUIT SLUMP

Fluffy dumplings in a hot fruit sauce served with cooling ice cream make a melt-in-the-mouth dessert.

1kg mixed soft fruit, such as blackberries, blueberries, raspberries and strawberries, defrosted if frozen
1 tablespoon caster sugar

FOR THE DUMPLINGS
250g self-raising white flour
A pinch of salt
1 tablespoon caster sugar
25g butter, diced

1 egg, lightly beaten
75ml skimmed milk

TO SERVE
4 tablespoons low-fat iced dessert or natural yoghurt

PREPARATION TIME 10 minutes
COOKING TIME 30–35 minutes
SERVES 4

1 Pick over the fruit, rinse it if necessary and place it, still damp, in a wide, deep frying pan or large saucepan, then add the sugar and stir. Cover the pan and simmer the fruit over a low heat for 15 minutes, shaking the pan or stirring frequently to prevent the fruit sticking. As the fruit slowly simmers, it should 'slump', or soften, into a textured sauce. **2** Meanwhile, to make the dumplings, place the flour in a mixing bowl and stir in the salt and sugar. Rub in the butter until the mixture resembles breadcrumbs, then quickly stir in the egg and milk to make a dough. Divide the dough in half and shape each half into eight walnut-size dumplings – a total of 16. **3** When the fruit has simmered into a sauce, drop the dumplings into it, spacing them as far apart as possible. Cover and continue simmering for 8 minutes, then turn the dumplings over, cover again and simmer for a further 8 minutes. **4** Serve four dumplings per person with a little sauce, accompanied by a tablespoon of low-fat iced dessert or natural yoghurt.

NUTRIENTS PER SERVING KCAL 392 • CARBOHYDRATE 73g (of which 22g sugars) • PROTEIN 11g • FAT 8g (of which saturated fat 4g) • FIBRE 6g • SODIUM 402mg • SALT 1g • FRUIT PORTION 3

Apricots need to be completely ripe to be eaten raw. Dried apricots, though high in sugar are a good alternative.

EVE'S PUDDING WITH CREAMY ORANGE SAUCE

Apricots and apples are topped with a light sponge with walnuts and almonds for a nutty texture.

200g ready-to-eat dried apricots, cut into chunks
4 Cox's apples, peeled, quartered, cored and
   thickly sliced
100ml unsweetened apple juice
2 eggs
50g caster sugar, plus extra for dusting
50g plain flour
85g almonds, coarsely ground or very finely
   chopped

FOR THE ORANGE SAUCE
Grated zest of 1 orange and juice of 3 oranges
2 tablespoons cornflour
2 tablespoons sugar
280g low-fat crème fraîche

PREPARATION TIME 20 minutes
COOKING TIME 1 hour
SERVES 6

1 Heat the oven to 200°C (400°F, gas mark 6). Put the apricots and apples in a 1.4 litre ovenproof dish, 7.5cm deep. Add the apple juice, cover and bake for 30 minutes. Leave to stand, uncovered, while you prepare the sponge topping. **2** Whisk the eggs with the sugar until very pale, thick and creamy. Sift in the flour and add the almonds. Using a large metal spoon, fold the flour and nuts into the mixture until incorporated. **3** Pour the sponge mixture over the fruit, spreading it evenly to the edge of the dish. Bake for 30 minutes, until the topping is risen and browned. Dust with sugar. **4** Make the orange sauce about 5 minutes before the pudding is cooked. Pour the orange juice into a jug and add water to make it up to 300ml. **5** In a small saucepan, mix the cornflour and sugar to a smooth paste with the orange zest and a little of the diluted juice. Gradually stir in the remaining juice. Bring to the boil, stirring continuously, then simmer for 2 minutes, still stirring. Remove from the heat. **6** Stir in the crème fraîche and transfer to a warmed jug. Spoon the pudding into bowls and serve with the orange sauce.

NUTRIENTS PER SERVING KCAL 360 • CARBOHYDRATE 51g (of which 39g sugars) • PROTEIN 7g • FAT 15g (of which saturated fat 5g) • FIBRE 4g • SODIUM 56mg • SALT 0.1g • FRUIT PORTION 1

FLUFFY BANANA RICE PUDDINGS

A light milk pudding is sweetened with honey and bananas for a nutritional boost. It is a great alternative to a simple nursery favourite.

60g short-grain pudding rice
600ml semi-skimmed milk
3 tablespoons clear honey
1 vanilla pod
2 ripe bananas
Finely grated zest of ½ lemon
2 egg whites

A pinch of freshly grated nutmeg

PREPARATION TIME 10 minutes
COOKING TIME 1 hour 15 minutes -
  1 hour 45 minutes
SERVES 6

1 Place the rice in a saucepan with the milk, then stir in the honey and add the vanilla pod. Bring gently to the boil, then reduce the heat and cover. Simmer for 1 hour–1 hour 15 minutes, stirring occasionally to prevent it sticking, until the rice is soft and the mixture has thickened but is still sloppy. **2** Meanwhile, heat the oven to 200°C (400°F, gas mark 6). Remove the vanilla pod from the rice. Peel the bananas and slice them thinly, then fold them into the rice with the lemon zest. **3** In a clean, dry bowl, whisk the egg whites until soft peaks form. Fold them into the rice mixture, then spoon it into six 200ml ramekins, or a 1.2 litre soufflé dish, and sprinkle with nutmeg. **4** Place the ramekins or dish on a baking sheet and bake individual puddings for 10–12 minutes, or the large pudding for 25–30 minutes, until golden brown and well risen. Serve warm.

NUTRIENTS PER SERVING KCAL 141 • CARBOHYDRATE 26g (of which 17g sugars) • PROTEIN 5g • FAT 2g (of which saturated fat 1g) • FIBRE 0.5g • SODIUM 65mg • SALT 0.16g • FRUIT PORTION 0

HOT RASPBERRY SOUFFLÉS

Raspberries give these individual desserts a beautiful, soft rose colour and a delectable flavour. They must be eaten straight from the oven to capture their deliciously light, melt-in-the-mouth texture.

10g unsalted butter, at room temperature
115g caster sugar, vanilla flavoured or plain
250g fresh raspberries
1 tablespoon kirsch, optional
4 large egg whites
1 tablespoon icing sugar, for sifting

TO SERVE Double cream

TOTAL TIME 25 minutes
SERVES 4

1 Before you sit down to your main course, preheat the oven to 190°C (375°F, gas mark 5). Grease the insides of four 200ml soufflé dishes, or ovenproof cereal bowls, with the butter, then coat them evenly with some of the caster sugar, tipping out any surplus, and place on a baking tray. **2** Purée the fresh raspberries by pressing them through a stainless steel or nylon sieve with the back of a spoon. Stir in the kirsch, if using. **3** When you have finished the main course, whisk the egg whites with an electric beater until they are stiff but not dry, then gradually whisk in the remaining caster sugar. Keep whisking until the mixture becomes shiny. **4** Carefully fold the raspberry purée into the egg whites, then spoon the mixture into the dishes and make a swirl on top of each. Cook in the centre of the oven, leaving space above for the soufflés to rise, for 12–14 minutes, or until well risen and lightly set. **5** Remove the soufflés from the oven, sift icing sugar evenly over the top of each and serve immediately, with cream.

NUTRIENTS PER SERVING KCAL 174 • CARBOHYDRATE 37g (of which 37g sugars) • PROTEIN 4g • FAT 2g (of which saturated fat 1.5g) • FIBRE 1.5g • SODIUM 80mg • SALT 0.2g • FRUIT PORTION 0

A

CONVERSION CHART

All food in the UK is now sold in metric units so it makes sense to cook using these measurements. If you feel happier using imperial measurements, you can use the chart below. Remember to use either metric or imperial and don't mix the two.

WEIGHT		VOLUME	
METRIC	IMPERIAL (approx)	METRIC	IMPERIAL (approx)
5g	⅛oz	30ml	1fl oz
10g	¼oz	50ml	2fl oz
15g	½oz	75ml	2½fl oz
20g	¾oz	85ml	3fl oz
25g	1oz	90ml	3¼fl oz
35g	1¼oz	100ml	3½fl oz
40g	1½oz	1 litre	1¾ pints
50g	1¾oz		
55g	2oz		
60g	2¼oz		
70g	2½oz		
75g	2¾oz		
85g	3oz		
90g	3¼oz		
100g	3½oz		
1kg	2lb 4oz		

VEGETARIAN COOKBOOK was published by the Reader's Digest Association Limited, London from material first published in the Reader's Digest books: **Thirty Minute Cookbook**, **Low Fat No Fat**, **Great British Dishes the Healthy Way** and the series **Eat Well, Live Well**.

First edition copyright © 2006
The Reader's Digest Association Limited
11 Westferry Circus, Canary Wharf,
London E14 4HE
www.readersdigest.co.uk

Reprinted 2010

We are committed both to the quality of our products and the service we provide to our customers. We value your comments so please do contact us on **08705 113366** or via our website at **www.readersdigest.co.uk**

If you have any comments or suggestions about the content of our books you can contact us at **gbeditorial@readersdigest.co.uk**

Project Editor **Lisa Thomas**
Copy editor **Jill Steed**
Designer **Jane McKenna**
Nutritionist **Fiona Hunter**
Indexer **Michael Dent**

READER'S DIGEST GENERAL BOOKS
Editorial Director **Julian Browne**
Art Director **Anne-Marie Bulat**
Head of Book Development **Sarah Bloxham**
Managing Editor **Nina Hathway**
Picture Resource Manager **Sarah Stewart-Richardson**
Pre-press Account Manager **Dean Russell**
Product Production Manager **Claudette Bramble**
Senior Production Controller **Katherine Tibbals**

Origination **FMG**

Printed and bound in China

Book code 400-314-02
ISBN 978 0 276 44211 7
Oracle code 250005137S.00.24